## *OPEN UP A MARVELOUS WORLD OF LEARNING AND FUN, AT HOME, IN YOUR BACKYARD— EVERYWHERE!*

**PARENTIPS** is your idea book and how-to guide to hundreds of child-pleasing games like:

**Water Slide:** For summer fun, a homemade water slide is great entertainment for the neighborhood. . . .

**Rainy Day Fun:** Make a "Rainy Day Box" and keep it strictly reserved for rainy days. . . .

**Dollhouse:** A wonderful dollhouse can be made with four boxes. . . .

**Company's Coming:** A home drama which teaches good manners is to have a company meal *without* guests. . . .

**Camp Indoors:** Put up a card table and throw a sheet or blanket over it to make a delightful tent. . . .

**Sandbox Chemistry:** Show your child how to make a "real" volcano in a sand mountain. . . .

**Constellations:** On a clear, wintry night, bundle up warmly and take blankets or sleeping bags to an open field away from city lights. Have a private star watching party. . . .

# PARENTIPS

*Quality Time with Kids*

## Bonnie Burgess Neely

PUBLISHED BY POCKET BOOKS NEW YORK

Another *Original* publication of POCKET BOOKS

POCKET BOOKS, a division of Simon & Schuster, Inc.
1230 Avenue of the Americas, New York, N.Y. 10020

ISBN: 0-671-60782-0

First Pocket Books printing June 1987

10 9 8 7 6 5 4 3 2 1

# Contents

# Acknowledgments

I want to express my appreciation to Susan Swint, the remarkable mother of six outstanding children. Susan has been my "behind-the-scenes" co-writer since the beginning of my newspaper feature, *Formulas for Fun*, many years ago.

At deadline time each month, when I am frantically working at the typewriter, she calls me with more excellent PARENTTIPS. This book is a tribute to my dear friend who is the kind of tireless, always smiling, model parent that we would all like to be.

I would also especially like to thank my father and mother, Mr. and Mrs. James F. Burgess of Greenville, S.C., whose parenting is reflected in the pages of this book.

Two people in my growing up years frequently encouraged me to become the professional writer that I had always dreamed of being. Unfortunately, they have passed away. But I want to dedicate this book to them, the late Mrs. P. N. Becton and the late Mrs. Richard L. Branyon.

A *very special* thanks to Mr. Rhea T. Eskew, who believed in a would-be writer, took the time to show her how to become a professional, and gave her the opportunity to do so.

Thank you to the many readers of *Formulas For Fun* who made this first book of PARENTTIPS possible.

# Introduction

PARENTIPS is a book a busy parent can grab for a quick idea and say to a crying four-year-old, "Here's something fun we can do together now while I'm doing my work." This is also a book you can give your teenager who has watched too much TV and say, "You'll find something in here that is more fun to do!" This book is for parents with children of any age. It shows you how to incorporate meaningful time *with* your children into a daily routine that may be too busy to yield *time out* for them.

I wrote PARENTIPS at the request of many readers of my syndicated newspaper feature, *Formulas For Fun*. Hundreds of their ideas are compiled here to help you make your family times enjoyable experiences that stimulate creativity and establish learning as a fun way of life. PARENTIPS helps you strengthen family ties, and build happy memories.

"Family," as used in the book, is the unit in which the child lives. For a large percentage of today's children, "family" does not mean two parents. A parent who is struggling to make it alone, working long hours to make a living, will find many cost-free activities to enjoy doing with the children whenever a few moments can be spared. Single parents who have only weekends with their children will find innovative ideas for entertainment and for enjoying their children without always going to the movies or amusement parks. Senior citizens will also discover many interesting things to do with grandchildren.

Although the book was written with the family in mind, it will be useful in schools because the activities incorporate what's taught in art, science, reading, language, and physical education classes in lower grades. Students in the upper grades and in colleges will find numerous ideas for projects in home economics, science, child care, and elementary education courses. PARENTIPS is a valuable resource book for Scout leaders, teachers, baby-sitters, child care centers, and leaders of children's organizations.

As you and your children spend meaningful and enjoyable time together each day, your heartfelt interest in them along with your honest communication and love will build both a happy home and successful relationships with your children. The purpose of this book is not to teach you to be a perfect parent, because no one can be that. I wrote this to show you how you can really *enjoy* being with your children, to stimulate their natural abilities and creativity, and to make learning a way of life for them.

Creativity is not only the knack of making things, but also the ability to approach problems from a unique point of view and to find solutions to these problems that no one else has found. It is the ability to make an everyday, "ho-hum" activity sparkle with interest. I do not believe that creativity is a genetic gift from birth. Children *become* creative in stimulating environments that encourage them to experiment with their abilities and learn through enjoyable experiences. You don't have to be rich, or have an I.Q. of 150, or take a holiday in order to provide these experiences for your children. You only need to care enough to take the time to relate to them. PARENTIPS gives you many ideas on how to spend that time.

Time is, perhaps, the scarcest commodity in our busy world. But I believe it is the greatest privilege and most awesome responsibility to be given a new and innocent life to mold. Raising children is a 24-hour-a-day job, and the payment for this job, good or bad, lasts a lifetime.

The job bonuses of parenting are the thrill of feeling the soft tickle of fuzz as you caress your new baby's warm little head; the joy of seeing the excitement of your five year-old when he learns to ride a bike; the delight of tasting the birthday cake your nine year-old baked for you; the poignance of detecting cologne on your son's first-shaved chin; the wonder of hearing your teenager play an instrument you cannot play; the pride of watching your children grow into responsible, unselfish, capable citizens.

*Every* child is special. Say to each child, every day, "I love you." This important step gives your children security and develops in them a high sense of self-worth, which is the very best way you can equip them for happy, successful lives. Adults must express interest in children's academic and personal growth achievements and express affection daily. Laughing and playing as well as pleasant surprises should be part of the family environment.

Practice giving your child positive feedback. Spend time with each of your children every day, even if you can manage only five minutes at bedtime. Tell them with your words and by your body language that you are proud of them and that your love is unconditional.

Compliment them whenever it is possible, and be kind when giving "helpful" criticism. When you feel you need to correct your child, do it in a positive way, never conveying negative feelings about the child herself. For example, do not say, "Jane is bad to color on the wall." Say instead, "The wall is not for coloring. Let's clean it off and get some paper on which to color." Try to imagine yourself in your child's shoes, and then think before you speak. By instructing a youngster in nondamaging, positive ways, you will be much more effective.

How the child behaves and thinks will be affected by the images of himself that we present to him. From those closest to him, the child will formulate his own concept of who he is as a person. A positive attitude on the part of parents will lead to a child having warm personal relationships as he or she grows. Such a child will also be more keenly aware of his or herself and possess a greater understanding of others. Our goal should be to help a child develop a positive self-image and to learn how to project that image to others.

A child with a positive self-image is free to grow mentally and to experiment confidently with his abilities and interests, developing them to their fullest capacities. Children who grow up in an accepting, encouraging environment in which there is opportunity for learning and for creative expression will become productive, confident adults. In *ParenTips* you will discover how to make learning and creative thinking a way of life in your home. Learning is a joy in itself, and every activity in this book is geared to stimulate the learning process.

Giving our children happy memories and close, loving family relationships from which they can benefit throughout their lives, is what this job of parenting is all about. It is also our responsibility to open the door for continuous and rewarding personal growth for our children—physically, mentally, psychologically, and spiritually. And then, when the time is right, good parenting means encouraging our young men and women to assume adult responsibilities for a happy, productive life of their own.

# THE BUDDING ARTIST

E very child is a born artist! Encourage your child to develop his natural talent. Too many of us have been told when we were very young, "Don't make so many messes." "Be neat." "Keep the house clean." The nature of the creative process results in messes. Instead of admonishing your child about not making messes, teach your child from a very early age to clean up after himself.

Negative statements such as "You're not very creative," or directions like "Color in the lines," undermine a child's freedom of expression. A child who lives in an atmosphere of constant criticism learns to expect little of himself, as he is constantly falling short of what is wanted of him by others. Such a child is frustrated occasion after occasion and begins to develop low self-esteem. His poor attitudes about himself eventually hinder him. He attempts fewer and fewer new things, fearing that he will not be able to do them perfectly or that his accomplishments will be criticized. Eventually he will develop a fear of never being able to please anyone. He stops trying to think creatively and as a result his natural talents or artistic inclinations go unused. If nothing is done to change this unfortunate pattern of thought and behavior, the child may never demonstrate his or her natural creativity. How sad!

A child who lives in an atmosphere of appreciation and praise will gain confidence in himself and will be eager to try new things. However, it is not only necessary for the child to receive praise from his family, it is also vital for him to learn to congratulate *himself* on his accomplishments. Family will not always be around to give him a pat on the back. Therefore, encourage your child to look at his own efforts and say, "I'm proud of myself. I'm really learning!" or, "I've done this well." This will prevent your child from needing an audience in order to feel good about himself. It also reduces his dependence on the opinions of others. He will learn to feel comfortable with the fact that if something is done to his own satisfaction and pride, it is well-done. If the child lives in an atmosphere of appreciation, the process of learning or the creative activity that he is involved in will bring him joy.

As you read this chapter and try the ideas in it with your child, you will have the opportunity to create in your home an attitude of appreciation for the efforts of each member of the family, thus encouraging their creativity and the development of their natural talents.

## PREPARING FOR LITTLE ARTISTS

Provide your child with a space for messy projects, and never discourage his or her creativity. An ideal space for art would have a hard-surface, easy-to-clean floor, and would be near a sink. It would be in a place where the child can talk to other family members, but where the mess would not be visible to those who prefer neatness.

If you are able to build a place to those specifications, your child is lucky, indeed. If your budget is limited, you can create an art projects table from sturdy boxes or from an old table that you could find at a junkyard or a garage sale. You can make a satisfactory table by placing an old, plain door on two saw horses or oil barrels. Telephone wire spools (from your phone company) also make wonderful small tables for children's art projects.

If you can afford to have a professionally built art area, consider an "L" shaped desk-height bar cabinet on rollers. It should fit in the corner of a room and have a wall about twelve inches above its washable counter surface, to hide a child's mess. This wall will also enable a child to see over it and communicate with others or watch TV while he creates, if he wants to do so. Drawers for supplies are vital. There should also be a space without drawers where your child can sit comfortably while he works and creates. If a chair or stool will be used, this space should be properly aligned with the position of the chair or stool. The bar should be placed near a bathroom or laundry area so that water is readily available.

## PROTECTING YOUR HOME

For most of us building an art area for a child is just a pipe dream. But there are several things you can do to make this dream a reality. First, protect your floor or carpet by getting a large piece of heavy cardboard from a store's dumpster. Or, if you can afford the nominal expenditure, purchase a piece of one-fourth-inch-thick clear rigid acrylic in a size that will cover the area in which your child will work. (This is also handy to place beneath a baby's eating chair, so you may be able to get two uses from your expenditure.) The clear plastic can be stored behind a couch or under a bed when not in use. It is advisable to have the corners rounded to prevent accidents.

## PROTECTING CLOTHING

The next important item to get is a good smock to protect your child's clothing. One of Dad's old shirts works nicely, or you might make a cover-all apron from inexpensive waterproof material. (Try making the apron from a shower curtain liner or a plastic tablecloth. These are inexpensive sources of a large amount of supple vinyl and can be machine-stitched without tearing.) Make sure the fabric is machine-washable.

If you don't sew, use a large waterproof pillowcase (available from a Sears catalogue or from medical supply stores) and cut out holes for a child's arms and neck. Split the center of one side so the apron will open down the back, if you want. You can also do this by using a plastic trash bag or a sturdy nylon duffel bag.

## SELECTING SUPPLIES

It is difficult to decide which art supplies to purchase from the endless number of supplies that are available. Basic "musts" include crayons and pencils ("fat" ones for children under five), a pencil sharpener, scissors (a pair appropriate for your child's age and whether or not he or she is a "lefty"), tempera paint, one large and one small quality paintbrush, and paper. With these basic supplies your child can become quite an artist. Throughout this chapter you will discover other materials that you may want to add to your supply box.

Paper is expensive, but there are many free sources of it available if you are willing to make a few telephone calls. Call companies who manufacture business forms, and local newspapers. Ask if they normally throw away roll-ends or other paper. If so, you are probably more than welcome to collect it. Any business that uses a computer printer throws away lots of paper. You yourself discard more paper than you realize. Consider saving sacks, letters, envelopes, wrapping paper, cards, junk mail, butcher paper. Most of these have a blank side that is never used or have blank spaces which could be cut off and then used.

If you can afford to purchase art paper, one of the cheapest sources is a roll of non-glossy butcher paper. You are lucky if you can also afford to purchase a roll holder/cutter to mount on a closet wall, so you and your child can easily tear off whatever size paper he needs. If your child enjoys finger painting, you might pay just a little more to get the paper that is glossy on one side. A roll of butcher paper is a fairly major investment, but will last for years and save money in the long run.

If that purchase is too heavy an expense, look for white wrapping paper and shelf-lining paper (not the bug-proof kind!) on sale. Collect rolls as you can afford them.

Although most schools advocate using manila art paper, I believe it is unsatisfactory because it tears so easily. A better source of large sheets of inexpensive art paper is a tablet of newsprint, available at art supply counters in most discount stores. These sheets can be used as is, or cut in halves or fourths for easier handling.

An easel is a good purchase, and you can probably find

an inexpensive, used one by checking with local artists or college art departments. For large or flimsy pieces of paper, place a big piece of cardboard on the easel and use clothespins to hold the paper in place while the child paints.

## LEARNING ABOUT COLOR

You and your child will have fun learning about color together. Ask your child what his favorite color is and check a psychology book at the library to learn something about your child's personality from his choice. It's a very interesting subject that may give you new insight with which to observe your child (and yourself).

### MAKING PAINT

Powdered tempera is a better investment than the jars or palettes of color. Your children will enjoy helping you mix the powder with water for normal painting, or with liquid starch for finger painting. They can make it thick for rich color or thin with more water for paisleys. The powder, available at educational supply stores and some art suppliers, lasts for years, so you might split the purchase with several friends. Keep pimento and bouillon cube jars or baby food jars for the paints you mix. It would be safer to collect small plastic containers with air-tight lids, such as yogurt or margarine containers, or large plastic pill bottles. The paint will last longer if you use sterile water to mix it.

---

If you purchase red, blue, and yellow, plus white and black, you can mix any shade or color your child desires.

---

### PRIMARY PIGMENT COLORS

Teach your child the three primary pigment colors: red, blue, and yellow. Tell him that he can get new colors by mixing these colors and show him how to mix them. Have him experiment with his paints.

## MAKE A COLOR WHEEL

A color wheel is useful in teaching the child many things about color. Help him make a color wheel to hang in his art center for constant reference and learning. He should place a large blob of each primary color on the paper as the points of a triangle.

Between the points, tell him to mix the two colors together and see what color he gets. For instance, between yellow and red he would produce orange, between red and blue he would produce purple, and between blue and yellow he would produce green. He should mix equal portions of each color for the first experiment. Teach him that these three new colors he has created, green, orange, and purple, are secondary colors.

With a pencil and ruler, have the child draw straight lines to connect the primary colors in the shape of a triangle. Draw other lines to connect the secondary colors in another triangle, making a six-pointed star on the paper. Connect all the colors in a circle, which is the color wheel.

## WARM COLORS

Talk to your youngster about warm colors. Have him describe the colors in fire, by really observing the reds, oranges, and yellows. Ask him what other things have warm colors (the sun, stove burner, fall leaves, etc.). Ask him why they are called "warm colors."

## COOL COLORS

Observe cool colors in nature by looking at grass, sky, lakes, mountains. Ask him to name the cool colors: blue, purple, green, and to name other cool things in these colors.

## TERTIARY COLORS

When your child has learned about primary and secondary colors and he understands well the principles of color mixing from the experiments you have done together (see above), he is ready to learn about tertiary colors, which are formed by mixing unequal portions of two of the primary colors to form yellow-green, blue-green; or red-purple and blue-purple; or red-orange and yellow-orange. Help him experiment by mixing from dollops of secondary and primary colors all around his color wheel. (See above.)

## MAKING BROWN

On the paper your child will have fun creating brown by mixing equal portions of all three primaries. Show him brown can also be produced by mixing equal portions of all three secondary colors. Ask the child to figure out why this is true. (Answer: Because the secondaries are made from equal portions of the primaries.)

## EXPANDING PAINT SUPPLIES

Using the tempera primary colors mixed with just a little water, have your child experiment to see if he can produce the secondary and tertiary colors in jars to keep and use as he paints. Even very young children can do this successfully and learn about color mixing. Use a measuring spoon to get equal portions of color for secondaries and unequal portions for tertiaries. You will be teaching measuring, pre-math concepts, and pre-science concepts, as well as art. Your child will never suspect the process is an educational lesson at all. To him it will be pure magic! (Note: Do not add water to dilute these colors in the jars.)

## TINTS AND SHADES

As the child grows and understands about color, he can use crayons or the jars of thick paint he has mixed (see above) to learn about tints and shades of color. Tell him that colors without black or white are called "pure" or "hues." By adding white to any hue, he will achieve a "tint" of that color.

Experiment by making a dot of each pure color across the bottom of the page. (It is very important to wash the paintbrush between each color so you have no contamination. Or use a separate cotton swab for each hue.) In the row above these colors, have the child mix a little white with each color to see the tint that is achieved. On the next row above, mix more white with each, and on successive rows upward until the top row is almost pure white, just barely tinted with the colors. It is easier for the child to remember, "for tints, add white" if the chart moves upward as the colors get lighter, because light is associated with the sky.

For learning about shades, the pure colors should be placed at the top of the page. As the child adds varying amounts of black to create shades of the hues, he can make his chart going down the page with each row of darker colors until almost pure black is reached. To help him remember which are shades and which are tints, tell him to remember that the shade from a tree when it falls on grass looks black-ish and that shadows are dark. "For shades, add black."

## COMPLEMENTARY COLORS

As the child gets older, teach him about complementary colors. These are colors which are opposite each other in a color wheel: red-green; orange-blue; purple-yellow. Note that in each pair of complementary colors you have one primary color and the secondary color which is formed when you mix the other two primary colors, thus complementing or completing the color spectrum.

Now teach your child a real magic trick. He can always be sure of the complementary color because his eyes will tell him. He should stare at a pure primary color for a few minutes, perhaps a sheet of construction paper. Then have him look immediately at a white paper or white wall or simply close his eyes. He will see the image of the object again but this time it will appear in the complementary color! More natural magic!

For the young child use only large-size art tools—"fat" crayons and pencils, large brushes and paper—to help him develop control of his larger muscles. Although learning to color within the lines of a coloring book teaches hand-eye coordination, it limits creativity. Blank paper is much better for art purposes. (See chapter "Hooking the New Reader.")

## COLOR ACTIVITIES AND PLAY

Teach your child that pictures do not have to be imitations of anything. Tell him that many famous artists use color for the joy of the color itself, not to paint a picture of something realistic. Your child will be freer in his self-expression and experimentation with art if he understands this from the beginning.

When the child shows you his creation, do not say, "What is it?" That implies both that art *has* to represent some real object and that your child has failed in that attempt because it is unrecognizable. This question discourages the child. Instead, say to the child, "This is a really interesting picture. Tell me about it." Take time to look appreciatively at the picture and congratulate the child on his efforts. Display the picture in a place where everyone can see it for a few days. Ways of displaying it are at the end of this chapter.

Children learn by playing. There are many ways your child will enjoy experimenting with color. He will see the results and draw his own conclusions as some activities are repeated and new ones added. Read on to learn how to give your child hours of fun. He will be learning without even suspecting it!

### PAINT GUNS

Fill several squirt bottles or water guns with watery tempera paint. Hang some art paper outside on the clothes-line or pin it to a tree. The child can create amazing pictures and have lots of fun by squirting the paints at the paper. Several children in old clothes or swimsuits will enjoy paint-ing each other this way too. Tempera paint will wash off with the garden hose or a good bath.

### SLING PAINTING

A fun free-form painting can be made by slinging paint onto paper. Have the child hang the paper outside in a place where the paint won't harm anything, should it miss the paper. Use thick tempera, about the consistency of cream. Dip large paintbrushes into the paint and simply sling the paint in the direction of the paper. Various colors will overlap and blend to form interesting images.

## NATURE SPATTERING

Your child can spatter paint, outdoors, to produce images of leaves, etc. Have him place several leaves on a sheet of construction paper. The paper should be on a well-protected surface and the child should be in old clothes. Dip a toothbrush into paint or white shoe polish. Hold a piece of window screen about six inches above the leaves and paper. Rub the color-filled toothbrush over the screen until the paint has splattered over the entire piece of construction paper in an array of little spots. Remove the leaves and their images will remain.

## EYE-DROPPER PICTURES

Eye-dropper painting encourages freedom of expression. Lay the paper on a protected surface and give the child a medicine dropper or a small ear syringe to make droplets of color all over the paper. With this method he has some control over the image, yet it promotes free form.

## BLOW PAINT

Place a blob of watery paint on a piece of fairly slick paper. Give the child a drinking straw. Before the droplet of paint dries on the paper, tell him to blow it with the drinking straw to make the color move around on the paper. Be sure he understands to *blow*, not *suck!*

## YARN PAINTING

Dipping fat yarns into various colors of paint and then sweeping the paper with the drippy yarns adds another dimension to art projects.

## MARBLE PAINTING

Pour thick paint into a dish. Dip a marble into the paint and then shoot or roll it across the paper. To keep the marbles from going everywhere, put the paper in a 9-by-13-inch cake pan to do the marble painting. Use other colors and repeat the process.

## WARM COLORING

This is a super impressive, simple, and fun project for kids of all ages; however, youngsters should be supervised because this method could be a little messy. The child should place his paper on an electric warming tray (*not* on a hot plate!), which is comfortably warm. Then he should proceed to use wax crayons and color the picture on the warm surface. The colors will melt slightly and blend together for a really unique effect.

If you do not have a warming tray, you can achieve nearly the same results in another way. Simply iron (on the lowest setting) over the backside of a finished wax crayon picture. (Be sure to protect your ironing board with several layers of paper towels.)

## FOIL PAINTING

To produce an unusual picture, help your child glue aluminum foil smoothly to a piece of sturdy cardboard. He can indent a picture or design in the foil by using an old ballpoint pen or blunt pencil. Paint the entire background with black acrylic paint thinned to the consistency of cream. When this is dry, paint the lines of the picture or design with any color desired. Allow about an hour to dry. The child can then scratch the paint from the places where he wishes to reveal the silver. The entire painting will have a striking, shimmery effect. Spray it with clear acrylic spray in order to retard peeling.

## DYEING TO EXPERIMENT

Using dye is a good way to experiment with color. You can purchase special paper (Dippity Dye is the brand name) for children's dye projects. This paper promotes the spreading of the dye and dries satisfactorily. If you don't want the expense of special paper, simply use white paper towels and food coloring.

## AFTER-EASTER FUN

After your children finish dyeing Easter eggs, have them use the leftover egg dye to paint pictures. Before they begin, tell the children that, as they paint, these magical pictures will change and look a little different from what the child intended.

On a protected surface, have the children paint on paper towels with a brush to get unique paisley pictures that look like something they might dream. Encourage imaginative discussion of how the bleeding of the colors changes the originally intended images.

## DIP DYEING

Have your child fold a paper towel into a small square and dip each corner into one color. He can open the towel to inspect his design. Then re-fold it along other lines and dip the new corners into other colors. He can overlap or separate colors as desired. When he has finished dyeing a piece of paper, have him place it in a "sandwich" of newspapers to blot. Remove it from the newspapers and hang or lay flat on other papers to dry. When the dyed papers are dry, he can hang them as posters or use them to wrap gifts. He can also experiment with any crumpled, absorbent paper with a high rag content (watercolor paper or expensive stationery). This high-quality paper can be used as stationery after it is dyed.

## BATIKS

Batik paintings are easy and fun. Children will enjoy experimenting with fabric dyes to decorate T-shirts, or to create pictures on pieces of old white sheets or other fabric.

In a large can which is resting in a pan of water, melt paraffin or beeswax. (Supervise carefully! Paraffin has the potential to cause a fire very quickly. Never set the paraffin container directly on the burner. Do not use a microwave oven.) The wax is used to block out areas you do not wish to take the dye.

When the wax is melted, remove the pan from the heat, but keep the can of wax standing in the pan of hot water so it will not harden again. To make a design, the child dips the paintbrush into the melted wax and paints a simple picture on the fabric to be dyed. When the cloth is dipped into the color, the part where the paraffin is will not be dyed.

You can then set the dye according to directions on the fabric dye container. Remove the wax with hot water. Your children can make lovely batik wall hangings for their rooms, or turn the designs into throw pillows.

Older children may want to do a batik with more than one color. To do this, have the child draw and color his pattern on paper. Then draw his design on fabric with a pencil, lightly, because the pencil marks will not wash out. If the dyes to be used are red and yellow and the fabric is white, he should use wax to block out all areas that are to be white and red, and dye first only the ones to be yellow and orange in the final design. After dyeing these areas yellow, setting the dye, and washing out the wax, he should wax all areas he wants to remain yellow or white in the complete design. When he dyes the remaining fabric red, the areas turning orange will result from the red dye overlapping the yellow in the unwaxed yellow areas. When this dyeing is set, the remaining wax can be removed to result in a batik of red, orange, yellow, and white. Black embroidery pens can be used to outline the designs.

## BANNERS

Have the child create a unique banner by using the dye with a paintbrush. Lay a square piece of sheet material flat on a card table. Paint a bold design at the bottom of the square. Then move to the next side of the table and paint the same bold design again at the part of the fabric nearest you. Move around the table and repeat the design two more times. The result will be an interesting, nearly mirror-image, four-way design. The child can staple a wooden dowel to the top and bottom edges and hang the design on his wall with a piece of colored yarn.

## PRINTING

Printing experiments can give great satisfaction to your children. They will enjoy being able to make the same picture or design repeatedly. Below, you will discover several ways you can teach your child to gain skills in printing images. All of these are fun and the ones you choose will depend on your child's age and ability. For little ones, help with the cutting. Caution older children to observe safety rules when using knives.

## VEGETABLE PRINTER

Help your youngster cut a firm vegetable, such as a potato, in half. With a pencil the child should draw a simple design on the potato's cut surface. Then use a small paring knife to cut away about one-fourth-inch of the potato all around the lines of the design. For very young children you should do the cutting or give them only strong plastic knives to attempt it themselves. When the cutting is finished, the child can dip the potato printer into ink or acrylic paint and use it as a printer.

## PLASTIC FOAM PRINTER

Meat trays from the grocer are another item to use for printing. Wash them and trim off the edges, so they are flat. Then help your child carve her design into the flat bottom of the tray with a blunt tool so that the tray is not cut all the way through. A blunt pencil or the wrong end of a ballpoint pen works nicely. Cuts should be about one-fourth-inch wide. Use this design as you did the potato for printing. Because the child carves the design into the printer, it will be left blank in the print, and the background will be imprinted as color. This is the reverse of the process used with vegetable printing above, in which the object itself is printed because the background is carved away.

## LINOLEUM BLOCK PRINTING

Help your child make a picture by using the process of linoleum block printing on high-quality paper. This is also a good project for children to make their own, personalized Christmas cards or stationery. Use a linoleum block purchased from a craft or art store to cut or etch a design. Roll water-soluble ink onto the linoleum block with a brayer (roller). You can use the same block to print the design repeatedly. It can also be washed and stored for future use.

Tell your child before he begins to carve his design into the linoleum block that the print he makes from it will be backward from (or a mirror image of) the one he cuts into the linoleum block. To prevent disappointment, have him first draw his design on a piece of paper, then hold it up to a mirror to see the way it will appear in the print. He should make any alterations desired, then use carbon paper to copy the design onto the block.

## WORDS FOR PRINTING

If your child wants to print words, he must prepare his printer with letters and words written backward, since the print will be a mirror image (reverse) of the block printer. There is a simple and fun way to make the pattern for the backward letters and words.

For linoleum block printing (see above) the child should use a piece of paper cut to the size of the linoleum block. After drawing the design and writing the words on the paper exactly as he wants the finished print to be, he should place a piece of carbon paper beneath his paper design, but turn the carbon the "wrong way" (so that it will leave the copy on the back of his original design instead of on another piece of paper) and mark firmly his entire design again, over all the original lines, including the words. The carbon will leave the backward impression of his design on the back side of the paper.

Now have him place the carbon paper on his linoleum block, so that the carbon impression will be made on it. Place his paper pattern on top of the carbon paper so that the backward design is toward the child. He must retrace all the lines firmly, so the backward impression is the resulting design on the linoleum block. Help him carve all the lines into the linoleum. When he prints on paper, the letters and words will read correctly.

The same method of preparing the block for printing can be used on any flat-surfaced, smooth wooden block instead of a commercial linoleum block. Carving tools, or a knife, screwdriver, or chisel can be used to cut the design into the wood.

# PICTURES WITHOUT PAINTBRUSHES

Typically we think of art as using paintbrushes and paper, but
you and your child can discover many ways to create exciting
pictures. Read on to learn how.

## FINGER PAINTS

Some children adore the messy feeling of finger paints,
and some hate it. If your youngsters want to try, by all means
the simplest and easiest way is to use the dry tempera
powder mixed with liquid starch. Kids can finger paint on
glossy butcher paper. There are several other ways that are
fun to finger paint when little ones are tired of doing the same
old thing.

## GELATIN PAINT

Try softening gelatin dessert mix in a little hot water.
When cool enough, let children use it on shelf paper to finger
paint, or even directly on a white plate or the counter. It's fun
to do and they can lick their fingers clean. This is a good way
for the child who declares that finger painting is too messy to
enjoy the sensual fun of squishing paint.

It's also great for a toddler to do "just like big sister."
Put the toddler in his high chair to finger paint with gelatin
directly on the tray, while older siblings use regular finger
paints without interference from the little one.

## DETERGENT PAINT

You can have really clean fun with finger painting by
mixing dry tempera with liquid detergent. Have the child
finger paint directly on the countertop or bathtub walls. (See
chapter on Baths.) Since painting on walls and furniture is
normally forbidden, this is super fun. However, detergent
painting could prove confusing to a child not old enough to
understand that this one practically cleans itself up!

## GOO PAINT

"Goo Paint" is a nifty mixture of equal parts of flour,
salt, and water, with food coloring added to achieve the

desired hue. Help the child put the mixture into a squeeze bottle (like a catsup dispenser) and squeeze out a picture on paper. It will dry to a slightly raised design.

## NOODLE ART

Cooked spaghetti is an amazing art medium. Do not rinse it so that it will be sticky enough to adhere to paper wherever it is placed. The child can wiggle it around into any desired shape on paper and it will remain in place when dry. It can be left the natural color, or later painted with a cotton swab dipped into thick tempera.

## MOSAICS

Your child can make pretty mosaic pictures by drawing or tracing a picture from a coloring book. With a pencil help her mark off sections on the picture, like puzzle pieces. (Keep sections large in size and few in number for young children.) She should cover one section with a thick coat of white glue and use tweezers to place one color of the mosaic pieces. Items from your kitchen will work nicely: popcorn, rice, dried lentils, macaroni, small nuts, eggshell pieces; even salt and pepper or cake decorations can be sprinkled on. Colored rocks for an aquarium also work well. Help her select items of different colors for each different section of the mosaic.

Older children might prefer to do a mosaic with bits of broken glass or fabric scraps. Or kids can cut one-fourth-inch strips of colored paper and roll them up into tight spirals to place in mosaic sections.

---

To do a picture entirely with one type of object, for instance rice, macaroni, or grated coconut, you can paint it after the glue is dry, or you can dye the kernels before using them. To dye them, pour a little rubbing alcohol and food coloring into a glass jar. Add the dry substance to be dyed. Put on the lid and shake vigorously. Pour into a strainer or colander to drain and then dry on paper towels.

## FABRIC ART

Your child will be delighted with three-dimensional high-lighting of any of his art works. Give him pieces of colored yarn cut to about twelve-inch lengths. He can dip these in glue and then outline his drawings with them. He can also glue fabric pieces onto the objects he has outlined with yarn, if he wishes to add more textures.

## COLLAGES

Collages are fun and can be done in many ways. For a group of children to make a joint project, hang a long strip of butcher paper on a protected wall. Let the children plan the mural, deciding whether it is to be an abstract medley of colors, textures, sizes, and shapes, or whether it is to be a realistic picture that tells a story. Give them magazines and catalogues to cut and tear, as well as fabric scraps, ribbons, colored paper, cotton, beads, buttons, cellophane, foil. By gluing these onto the paper they can achieve a marvelous mural, and the project can last all day.

Objects in an abstract mural should be overlapped and cut out as shapes of color or texture, not as realistic people or cars, etc. As the final stage of the mural approaches, children may want to emphasize shapes by outlining with yarn or colored markers.

For a story mural, the children should decide what they want the mural to say before beginning the picture. They can cut out realistic objects such as people, cars, houses, or animals from magazines and catalogues and place them on the paper to tell the story.

## MATCH DESIGNS

You and your child can make many attractive home decorations and designs by using wooden matches which have been lighted and immediately extinguished, so that the charred ends create a black pattern in your design.

This project is not recommended for a child who seems overly fascinated with fire. Of course, you do not want any child to play with matches. It is best for you to burn the matches all at once before giving them to the child. An easy way to do this is to place the matches, all pointing the same way, in a disposable metal pie pan, which you place in a fireplace, or put the matches in a large can placed in the sink or outside near a water faucet. Have a large pitcher of water handy.

Light the matches, which will all catch fire almost simultaneously, since the igniting ends are together. Immediately pour water to extinguish them because you want only the ends burned. When the matches are cool and dry, give them to the child for the project. It's a good time to talk about the dangers of playing with matches or fire.

Before the child begins to create the decoration, have her protect the counter and her clothes, because the blackened match ends could rub off and become messy.

For a wall hanging cut a piece of cardboard into any shape your child wants. Help her glue on the burned matches side by side until the cardboard is completely covered and the pattern of dark and light areas makes her design. In this way she can also decorate a wooden trivet or a box to hold trinkets or stationery. The finished project must be sealed with a clear sealer to prevent the charred matches from rubbing off as the object is used. This simple project is really impressive and professional looking when completed. And it is relatively simple for most school-age children to accomplish.

## COLORED TISSUE

Let your child try brushing a mixture of water and white glue onto bits of colored tissue paper and applying them as the colors on a picture he has drawn. For young children a successful picture might be a fall tree with colored tissue forming the leaves. The children can glue the tissue flat or roll it into balls to make three-dimensional, smaller leaves. An older child can overlap colors and outline some areas with crayons; then, perhaps, he can spatter paint or use India ink on some areas. Finally, he might paint over some finished areas with the glue mixture again. The results are marvelous!

## FABRIC ART DECORATIONS

Children will enjoy doing their art work on T-shirts, pillowcases, aprons, or other fabrics. Purchase a set of fabric embroidery pens in basic colors. There are many good brands, but the easiest to use are the felt-tipped ones. (I like the Glad Rags brand.) The colors are fun for your children to use and do not fade or bleed in the wash. When painting fabric, tell them to place cardboard or foil beneath the layer being painted so that the colors do not go through onto another layer. If painting a T-shirt, put the cardboard inside the shirt.

## LEARNING ABOUT SHAPES

The world of geometrical shapes will open doors to more artistic adventures for your young children. Here are some ways to teach them about shapes and some tricks that are fun to learn at any age.

### TRIANGLES

Remind your child of his tricycle, which has three wheels. Tell him a triangle has three sides. Help him make a triangle with his fingers, by placing his index fingers end to end and then touching thumbs end to end. Talk to your child about which objects are triangles. You might make cookies using a triangular cookie cutter, or let the child help you unfold the dough from a crescent roll can. The pieces come in triangular shapes.

Help your child learn to cut triangles from paper, by cutting across the corner. The child can cut large or small triangles in this way, depending on where he places the scissors.

### SQUARES

Tell your child that a square has four sides, all the same length. Talk about which objects around your home are square in shape. Since more objects are rectangular, talk about the differences in rectangles and squares.

Show your child that most pieces of paper are rectangular, but cutting a square from the rectangle is easy and fun. Give her any rectangular piece of paper. Help her fold it so that the left edge of the paper is brought up to lie on the top edge of the paper. She should crease the fold, forming a triangle. One part of the paper will protrude beneath the edge of the resulting triangle. Have her cut away this extra part of the paper. When the paper is unfolded, the child has a perfect square.

## CIRCLES

Young children will enjoy pointing out circles among everyday objects. A plate or your wedding ring might be the first things to show him when he is learning about circles. Help him buckle a belt so that it forms a circle on the table.

Explain to your child that there are several ways in which to learn to draw a circle. First give him a can or a plate, then have him place it on a piece of paper and trace around it with a pencil.

When the child is a little older, help him learn to use a compass, which is tricky to master. Have your child practice until he becomes proficient with this tool. Because variety store compasses are often inaccurate, it is worthwhile to purchase a good compass from an art or office supply store.

Then show the child how to make his own compass by using a piece of string and tying a pencil to each end of it. One pencil stands upright to be the center of the circle, like the point of the compass. The other pencil draws the circle. Explain that this is useful to know because sometimes he may need a circle larger than his compass can draw or he may not have a compass when he needs one. Ask the child to think of how the string compass works. Explain that it keeps the pencil at all times the same distance from the center. Another way to demonstrate this is in a sandy place. Have one child stand as the center of the circle, holding one end of a string. Another child holds the other end of the string, pulling it taut, and walks around, dragging his foot in the sand to draw the circle.

Show the child how to cut a circle by folding a square in half both ways (so that a cross is made by the folds). With the square folded, round off the corner point where there is no fold. With a little practice, the circles he cuts will be nearly perfect.

## CUTTING STARS

There are many times it would be useful for your child (or you) to know how to cut a perfect star. Here is a very neat paper-folding trick to know, which a reader of my newspaper column sent to me years ago. I have used it frequently. It only takes one cut with your scissors to make a perfect star from paper or fabric. Practice this repeatedly with your child until you can both do it without the diagram.

# STAR

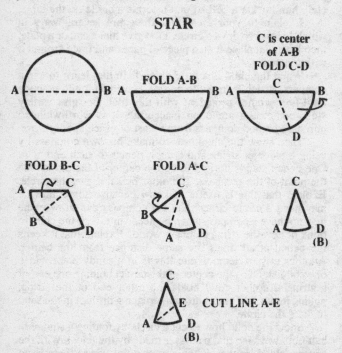

The best way to cut a star is by using thin, crisp paper or interfacing fabric such as thin Pellon. If you want the finished product to be of thicker paper or fabric, cut a pattern of the thinner material first and then trace the star pattern you have cut onto your thicker material.

Cut a circle the size you want the finished star to be. Fold the circle in half and crease the fold. (Fold A-B.) Fold the right side forward over the left side so that the folded piece is about twice as wide as the remaining uncovered pie piece. Crease this fold. (Fold C-D.) Fold the remaining pie piece flap backward and crease it even with fold B-C. Turn the folded paper over so the back is facing you. It should look like a tepee with a center flap (crease A-C) which forms a line down the center, visually dividing the tepee into equal halves. Fold the right side over the left side so this A-C crease is the valley of the fold; the two sides should match, with point B and point D together. Crease this final fold, which will be again at points A-C.

To make the star, cut from point A to point E. E can be at any place along line C-BD. If the cut is approximately in the middle of the line C-BD, the star will be a traditional shape. If E is closer to C, the points of the star will be slender. If E is closer to BD, the points of the star will be fat.

## SHAPE PICTURES

Have your child cut several different sizes of squares, rectangles, circles, triangles, and other shapes from different colors of paper. He can use these to make shape pictures. Ask him to use only squares and make a robot, use only circles and make a flower, use only rectangles and make an animal.

This project can be repeated with any geometric shape and also with holiday shapes like hearts, shamrocks, eggs, etc. Vary the activity by asking him to cut three triangles, five squares, ten circles, etc., and use all of them to make a person.

## ANYWHERE ART

Ask your child to cut various geometric shapes from colored felt. Tell her to place these, along with a five- by seven-inch rectangle of black felt, in a zipper plastic bag and hide the bag in your purse. Tell her that the next time she is waiting while you do errands she will have a fun, do-anywhere art project. She simply arranges the shapes she has cut on the black felt in any design, which she can rearrange as often as she wishes.

# TEACHING THE CHILD TO DRAW

For the youngster who wants very much to draw something realistic but does not like the results he achieves, here are some ways to offer help. Drawing is very different from the experiments in color and free-form art discussed earlier in the chapter. Drawing teaches the child to observe and reproduce on paper what he sees. For some children drawing is a favorite pastime, and you can hardly get them to stop for meals or homework. For others drawing can be very frustrating. Many of these children give up early, declaring they have no talent. But there are many enjoyable ways you can help to prevent this and encourage your child to learn to draw. A school-age child with average abilities can learn to copy simple shapes and make satisfactory drawings. You may even discover your own artistic talents in the process of doing these activities with your child.

## DRAWING OBJECTS

For a child who thinks she cannot draw, help her learn first to draw simple geometric shapes. When she can draw circles, squares, rectangles, ovals, and triangles, she is ready to draw anything she wishes, by learning to look at objects in a new way.

Tell her to draw a picture of a tree in this way: Have her look at the tree until she can see that the trunk is a rectangle and the top is a circle. Have her draw a rectangle with a circle on top, then modify the lines until they appear like the tree. This produces fun, cartoonish figures at first and takes lots of practice to master.

Show her how to draw stick figures for people. Help her remember to draw the initial, basic geometric shapes with very light marks, since the lines will be erased and redone as more filled-out figures.

A clown is a good figure to draw using shapes: a circle for the head with a triangle hat, an oval for the body, rectangles for legs and arms, ovals for feet and hands. Using this modified stick figure, the child can alter the lines to draw an identifiable clown. This technique teaches the child some very basic steps for drawing successfully.

## FEEL YOUR WAY

A fun way for a child to learn to draw is by "feeling with his mind's fingers." For this exercise, tell the child to look only at the object he's drawing, never at his paper. Using a pencil, he should quickly draw the outline of the object without ever taking up his pencil or looking at his paper. This blind contour drawing is a valuable artistic exercise for your child, and it frequently results in hilarious pictures that make the child think it is just a game.

## LOOK AT THE SUBJECT

When the child is learning to draw, his inclination will be to conjure up images and to try to put them on paper. Some children can easily do this and enjoy the results. But for the child who is not happy with his drawings, suggest that he make a game of having a contest with himself. Ask him to think of a toy he has which he would like to draw, perhaps a stuffed animal. Ask him to draw it as well as he can from memory and then give you the picture to hide.

Next, tell him to get the stuffed animal and a new piece of paper and to look at the animal as he draws it. When the picture is finished, bring out the first drawing. Ask him to decide which is better. The second drawing should be better than the first. If he says the second wins the contest, discuss the reasons why it might be better (because the child was drawing something he could see and he had practiced drawing it before).

Tell him he should draw objects which he can look at while drawing. Show him how he can visually divide the subject into segments and draw the basic geometric shape of each segment on paper, then carefully alter the lines a few at a time to achieve what he sees. The subject, of course, should be one which does not move.

---

If a child wants to learn to draw well he should draw something he sees every day, while looking at it. For teenagers, keep a drawing tablet by the telephone—they can sketch as they talk.

## SHADOWS

As your child becomes more adept at drawing the outlines of objects, have her notice the shadows and highlights on these objects. Shadows have shapes, too. If she will observe the shapes of the shadows and shade her picture with the correct shape of shadow, her pictures will take on a professional, three-dimensional look. Learning to see the shapes of shadows and highlights is difficult at first, because we are not accustomed to looking at lights and shadows but see only the total effect. Suggest that she play a game of first drawing only the shadows of an object she sees. When the shadows are complete she can add the rest of the object. She will be fascinated at her own drawing improvement.

## TWO PERSON PICTURE

There are many activities your child will enjoy and that encourage more freedom of line. For two or more children, a joint effort picture game is fun. One child draws an object on a piece of paper; for example, a mountain. The next child adds something else; maybe a person. The theme of the drawing develops with the picture, which continually changes as each child adds a new dimension. Each child adds something else to the picture until the drawing is completed to the satisfaction of all.

This drawing game can be varied by having the group agree before starting on which object to draw; perhaps, a car of the future. Each child in turn draws a few lines or a single part of the car until the picture is complete. The game is fun because each child will see a different car in his imagination, and when he adds part of that car, the next child is forced to rethink his own imaginary concept.

Another way to play the game, with often comical results, is to play it "blind." One child draws something on the paper and folds it over so that the other child cannot see what has been drawn. After a few verbal hints, the second child gets a turn to draw something on the paper, keeping the first drawing hidden. When his object is complete, he folds the paper and passes it to another child or back to the first. When all the paper is used up the children open it to see their picture. The results are often hilarious.

Three children can have fun drawing a person or an animal. No one knows what the other will draw. The first child draws a head and folds the paper back so that the second can draw a torso without seeing the head. The second child folds his drawing back and passes it to the third child, who draws the legs without knowing what the first and second children have drawn. The resulting picture is always humorous.

## SELF-PORTRAITS

By all means, have your young artists draw their own self-portraits at least once a year. A good way to do this is to make it part of the child's birthday ritual. It is also good entertainment during Christmas holidays. Keep these self-portraits and observe how they change through the years. If you wish, psychologists can give you helpful insights about your child's self-concept by interpreting these pictures. You can get clues as to ways you can help your child. Or you can keep them just for the fun of the memories.

"My Family" pictures are also great to have the child draw each year. These are such fun to look at together as the child grows up.

### FULL LENGTH PICTURES

The child will enjoy drawing himself full length, either from memory or in front of a mirror. He can do this on an average-size piece of art paper or on a very large piece of paper, if he would like to draw himself life size. (See "Me-Puppets" in the Index for other ideas.)

### BUST PORTRAITS

When your little artist needs a captivating project, have him draw his own face. Show him the self-portraits of famous artists. Norman Rockwell's is especially interesting to children. Place the child in front of a mirror and tell him to draw himself. Have him observe his own features carefully. Of course, the resulting portrait will be right-left reversed, because your child is observing a mirror image of himself. To teach him about mirror images, have him wear a T-shirt that has words on it. If he really draws what he sees in the mirror, instead of from memory, the words will appear backward on the drawing.

## DRAW A PHOTOGRAPH

At another time, have the child observe carefully a recent photograph of himself and draw or trace it. This is a difficult exercise and should be attempted only if the child will enjoy it and not be frustrated. We seldom look scrutinizingly at ourselves. The child might exclaim, "I never knew I had green in my eyes!" or, "My nose is shaped differently than I thought." It is a good self-awareness exercise and can occupy the youngster for a good while.

# PICTURE PROJECTS TO TRY

Children get tired of the same kinds of activities every day. Here are some innovative art projects which will stimulate interest and creativity while the child spends hours of fun.

## HALF PICTURES

For a special kind of drawing lesson, cut a large face from a magazine. It should be one with a full frontal view. Cut the face in half and mount one-half on a sheet of paper. Ask the child to draw the other side of the face. This can even be done with the child's own photograph. It's a good way to use one of those numerous duplicate school photos which tend to lie around in drawers for years because the child never got around to giving them away to friends. If you don't have one you are willing to sacrifice for the purpose, photocopy one in a copying machine for the art lesson. The larger the photograph, the better.

The activity can be varied by giving the child any half picture to complete. It could be an animal, a building, or a farm scene, whatever is handy. The purpose of this lesson is to sharpen the child's observation and to stimulate his memory.

## GIFT DRAWINGS

For a wonderful gift for someone she loves, have the child draw a picture of that person. She can stain or paint a wooden plaque, cut out her drawing, and mount it for hanging. Cover it with several coats of sealer.

If you have smaller children, mount all the drawings on the same plaque for a really unique gift for Mom, Dad, grandparents, or favorite babysitter. The gift will be treasured for a long time.

## SCRATCH ART

A really special drawing activity your child will enjoy and long remember is scratch art. He should use a piece of white paper and completely cover it with wax crayon colors, bearing down quite hard to make the colors thick. Color one area of the paper green, one blue, etc. Next have the child color over these hues with black, until the entire paper is thickly coated. Give the child a pointed object, such as a compass, a large needle, or a "dead" ballpoint pen. Have him scratch a design or picture through the black coating, revealing the colors beneath. It is a very effective picture.

You can also purchase "scratch art" paper from an art supplier. The child uses a stylus or sharp instrument to scratch a picture, with amazingly professional results.

## OIL PASTELS

As your children express themselves in art, stimulate their imaginations by purchasing a few additional supplies. Oil pastel crayons are especially rewarding to the young artist. These go easily onto paper and provide extremely rich colors. You and your children will enjoy playing with them and will be proud of the results. The special value of working with oil pastels is the ease with which colors can be blended.

## CURSIVE ART

Teach your child that his handwriting is a form of art he does every day, and it should reflect his best artistic abilities. Periodically, ask your child to write his name in his best handwriting (or printing) and display it as a work of art.

Your child can have fun making designs with his name. Give him a paintbrush to paint his name in very large letters, then fold the paper beneath the name, and blot it, so that when the paper is opened his name has made a mirror-image design.

## CALLIGRAPHY

Children old enough to write in cursive style will enjoy practicing the art of calligraphy. Get a book of instructions from your library and purchase a felt-tipped calligraphy pen in your child's favorite color. Encourage him to practice repeatedly, perhaps while watching TV or talking on the phone. This is a skill that could later earn him money, besides being rewarding simply as fun.

## DRAWING MAPS

Have a contest among your children to see who can draw the best map of your neighborhood or town. Award a prize for the winner and display her map on the family bulletin board. Beside it post an official map of the town, available at your local Chamber of Commerce. Announce that the map-drawing contest will be weekly, and see what improvements occur.

## MY STREET PICTURES

Expand their awareness by asking the kids to draw from memory a picture of their street with all the landmarks, buildings, largest trees, signs, mailboxes with names, etc., and to color them correctly. You may be surprised that, often, the youngest child has the most accurate observations.

## MIXED MEDIA

Mixed media experiments with your children can include any combination of two or more different kinds of media for producing a picture. Typically, children use pencils and crayons in the same picture. Suggest other ideas for mixed media and have fun working and playing with these along with your children.

## USING OIL-BASED COLOR

One word of caution: When using the method suggested here, first do a picture yourself to show your child what will happen. I made the mistake of washing my child's picture with paint thinner, thinking it would be a treat for him to see the magic results. He collapsed in tears, claiming I had smeared his best picture, because he had not first seen what to expect. An hour later, when the picture was dry, he was fascinated with its professional appearance and very delighted with the results.

While your child is watching, use oil pastel crayons to draw a picture on fairly slick paper. Fill in the outlined design with only partial coloring, leaving some spaces and the background white. Next use a soft graphite pencil, perhaps number 4B, to draw in the features and to emphasize outlines. These will be bold, very black lines. Finally dip a wide, soft paintbrush into paint thinner and paint it over the entire picture. The colors will blend and mute each other, while the spaces will be given a soft paisley color, turning your drawing, like magic, into a work of art suitable for framing.

When doing mixed media art, teach the children not to layer the work by using first the crayons, then the pencil, then last, perhaps, a wash. Use some crayon, then some pencil, then a wash, then *more* pencil, *more* crayon, etc. Adding the crayon and pencil *while the wash is still wet* makes unique and brilliantly smooth colors. By all means, be free and experiment. That's the fun of it! Work the picture, then rework it. Blend the colors by going over them in some areas. Your child will be so fascinated watching you that he will soon want to try his own picture.

## CHALK PASTELS

Chalk pastels are a wonderful addition to your art supplies. You and your children will enjoy using chalk pastels by themselves for creating pictures with a soft look. These are also wonderful types of color for use in mixed media.

Have the children create their pictures with chalk pastels on paper with a heavier rag content to prevent its buckling. A chalk pastel wash is done with water, not paint thinner. Because the chalk pastels produce a soft look, kids will probably use a lot of white to blend and mute the colors. It's a good idea to keep extra white on hand. When the coloring is finished the child can use a soft paintbrush dipped in water to wash over his painting for a unique, lovely effect. When the picture is thoroughly dry, spray it with a fixative to prevent the chalk from smearing. In a pinch, you can even use hair spray.

## DISPLAYING CHILDREN'S ART

To encourage the child's creativity and to show him you are proud of his creations, display the pictures he produces. (With all the ideas in this chapter, the art may be quite prolific.) Here are some ways that will help you make your child feel that his art is given proper attention. You might want to incorporate all of these ideas or choose one or two.

### MAGNETS

Give each child some good magnets and one section of the refrigerator surface for displaying his own art. Decorative magnets are usually not strong enough. Stronger ones can be purchased very inexpensively from an electronics store such as Radio Shack. Tell the children the display is up to them. They can change the pictures daily, hourly, or leave a favorite on display for weeks.

### FAMILY DISPLAY CENTER

Hang a large bulletin board in a central family area. Give each child a section of it and some push pins. He can change and display his own art as he chooses. It is a good idea to delineate the divisions with pieces of colored yarn, pinned into place, so there will be no fights over space. Give each child large fabric letters from a notions department of a fabric store to write his or her name on the board space.

### MAKING DISPLAY BOARDS

Your child may want to cover fiberboard with fabric to match the decor of his room. He can simply lay the fabric on one side of the fiberboard, allowing about six inches extra on all edges to pull to the back side and staple into place. The fabric not only makes the board a decorative touch, it also covers the ugly holes which result with repeated use of plain fiberboard as a bulletin board.

Your teenager may want to choose from some other ideas for bulletin boards, such as decorating one wall of his room with cork tiles or acoustical tiles, applied directly to the wall. (These are great for posters!) He could even use a piece of indoor-outdoor carpet, framed or applied directly to the wall.

## PIN-UPS

Your child can use straight pins to pin pictures directly onto a Sheetrock wall. Tell him to push the pins slightly downward instead of straight in. These will not leave visible holes that damage the wall, as nails and tacks do.

Children also enjoy using the gummy substance designed to hold posters on the wall. This will hold your children's art sheets securely without damaging your wall.

## FRAMES

One of the best ideas I have found is to purchase for each child several frames in different sizes, with a mat cut for each. These mats should take standard sizes of art paper, whatever sizes your children use regularly. Help the child cut a cardboard piece the size of the entire back of the frame and insert it as a backing for the pictures. Let him choose where to hang the frames. He can easily slip his artwork into the frame and tape it to the back of the mat, with masking tape, not cellophane tape. Your child can change his own artwork in his frame whenever he wishes. This eliminates the expense of having so many pictures framed through the years. It also eliminates the need to display all the art work in a special way. The child himself chooses his best, hangs it, and decides when to retire it.

## USING MATS

If you cannot afford frames, get a piece of black mat board from a picture framer. Have the outer edges cut professionally to appropriate sizes, but do not cut out the inner edges as normally done for a mat on a framed picture. Whenever your child has a picture to display, he can attach it to the center of this board, using poster gum bits or masking tape circles behind the picture. When he wants to display another picture, he simply removes the first one.

He may want to protect the picture by wrapping it with kitchen plastic wrap and taping the plastic over the back side. To the back of the board, help him attach a ring from a ring-pull can, using strong tape. The ring-pull is used to hang the board.

The same idea can be done by cutting the mat board as if for framing. Your child can insert the picture behind the cutout. If this way is used, you must have another cardboard to fit behind and sandwich the picture in place.

## ACRYLIC FRAMES

Children like the ease of displaying their art in flat acrylic frames. Kids might purchase in a discount store black mats in several different sizes to display art dramatically within a large acrylic box frame. Your children will also like using clear acrylic place mats which are made for the purpose of displaying children's art. These have a place to insert the picture, allowing the child to make his own place mat.

## RETIRING ART

Have your youngster keep a box under her bed or in her closet for retired art work or for any art the child feels she wants to keep but not display. Each summer help her select her best dozen to keep "forever." By then she will probably be ready to discard the rest.

## SEND TO LOVED ONES

If you have grandparents or other loved ones who live far away and want to stay in close touch with your children, have each child send them pictures frequently. If the child does not want to part with his best, help him photocopy or photograph it to send in the mail. Grandparents and the child, too, will be thrilled with the idea.

## COMPUTER ART

If your child has access to a computer with an art program, encourage him to learn how to draw in this magic way! It's even more rewarding if there is also a printer so he can keep what he draws and display it.

## PERSONAL STATIONERY

For a special surprise gift to reward your little artist, take your child's best artwork to a local printer and have it made into her own personal stationery. The youngster will be thrilled when she opens this special gift. She will be so proud of her stationery that she will want to write to everyone she knows. She might decide the stationery is good enough to package and sell on consignment in local stores. Your child may learn that art can be a business as well as a hobby.

# RAINY DAY FUN

I always get a very special, cozy feeling of happiness on rainy days. I believe it goes back to the time when I was a little girl. My mother kept a "Rainy Day Box" in the attic. It was the only time we children were allowed to play in the attic or to use the contents of that special box. How we loved going into that wonderful hideaway and hearing the rain dancing on the roof.

Make a "Rainy Day Box" for your children. Place in it some of your own childhood toys, if you can locate any. Old evening clothes for your kids to play dress-up are a "must" for the box. Be sure to include a purse, hats, heels, pantyhose, and jewelry. And put in some men's clothing for little boys.

There are also items you will want to purchase for your "Rainy Day Box." These include:

scissors
glue
felt-tipped washable markers
permanent markers
rubber bands and paper clips

various kinds of tape
colored pipe cleaners
wiggly plastic eyes for little animals
magnets
clothespins
construction paper
typing paper
pencils and crayons
crepe paper
aluminum foil
screwdriver and screws
hammer and nails

The contents of the "Rainy Day Box" may change from year to year, and what is in it is really not very significant. The important thing is that it is strictly reserved for special, rainy days.

## CREATING TRASH-CAN TREASURES

Things you normally throw away can provide hours of rainy day fun, if you remember to save the right items. Get a large cardboard box that you can keep in the attic, basement, a spare closet, or under the bed, and into it toss a few of the following trash items. Then, when your children need entertainment, you can provide novel, creative crafts.

Items to save include:

cardboard cylinders from paper towels and
        bathroom tissue
film cans
pieces of cardboard in varying weights
plastic chips and packing pieces
catalogues
disposable cups
corks
old jewelry
empty plastic containers of all sizes and shapes
bits of yarn, lace, fabric
all sizes of boxes, especially those with unusual
        shapes

potato chip cans
cans with plastic lids
used wrapping paper and ribbons
oatmeal and salt boxes
paper sacks
scraps of wood
string
spools
old socks
magazines

Once you get into the habit of looking through your trash for the purpose of making creative crafts, you will find all sorts of other items to save. But do not save more than one boxful at a time. When the kids have used up all those "goodies," you can save more. That way, you do not end up with a truckload of trash in your house.

## STIMULATE CREATIVE THINKING

Periodically hold up any everyday item for your children to brainstorm with. Tell them to pretend they are Beings from another planet who have just discovered this odd item (perhaps plastic foam cups) and are trying to figure out what it is. See how many different ideas your children can think of for using the cups creatively. They might suggest making the cups into toy binoculars, monster eyes, ear phones, building blocks, party hats, or megaphones. The cups could become part of a costume, such as animal horns or noses. The kids might suggest using the cup to write on, to carry or store objects in, to mold sand or gelatin, to make Christmas tree ornaments or Easter baskets, or for planting seeds. Cups could be glued together to make abstract designs or realistic sculpture, torn into confetti, used to shake dice, make a bird feeder, roll in a race, blow into the air, or make a bicycle obstacle course.

Regular brainstorming games like these will help your children learn to look at throwaway items as creative construction media. Remember, creative thinking carries over from making art projects into problem-solving in life.

## IMAGINATIVE PLAY

Your child can turn a large box into a spaceship, car, boat, or plane in which the child can be the pilot. Tell him to use spools and foil to create knobs and dials to guide his machine. Other boxes can be wings or seats.

## ROBOTS

Two boxes appropriately stacked and taped together make a wonderful, life-size robot for your child to animate by getting inside. Your child can also make smaller boxes into a little robot to use with little plastic toys. If your child is old enough, he may even make a movable robot by taping the boxes to a remote-control car. Perhaps he would want to make the robot talk by adding a small tape cassette voice. The creation can become very real looking when he glues foil all over the boxes.

## CASTLES

Your children will have fun taping together shoe boxes and other boxes of various sizes to make a castle. Add potato chip cans for towers, topped with inverted, cone-shaped paper cups. Small boxes can be attached for balconies and a box lid can become a drawbridge, worked by strings. Help the kids make flags to fly from the towers by drawing on bits of fabric with permanent markers. Youngsters can cut out shields and coats of arms from colored paper or foil.

If the children spend many hours making their castle quite elaborate, suggest that they paint it to look as though it were made out of stones. If the project is sturdy enough and your kids have a lot of patience, they could even glue on real pebbles with epoxy glue to make the castle look authentic. Or use decorator adhesive-backed paper that looks like stone or brick to make the castle something you and your children will want to save.

## DESERT SCENES

Children can build toy houses from boxes. Flat-topped houses are easy to make by turning shoe boxes upside down.

Help youngsters texture adobe walls with plaster of paris or instant papier mâché, which is available in craft shops.

Kids will enjoy constructing stairs on the outside up to the roof. A simple ladder can be made of sticks laced together with rope, or it can be made of small cardboard matchboxes stacked and taped together.

For the sandy desert, give the children a few sheets of sandpaper, or place the scene in a large flat box and surround it with real sand. For an oasis, they can use a small mirror for the water. Kids could make palm trees with brown construction paper cylinders for the trunks and green paper for fronds.

Your children may need a little help from you to create the all-important well. If your kids have never seen a real well, explain to them its purpose and how the water is drawn; also show them books with pictures of wells.

To make a delightful and functional toy well, kids can cover a rigid plastic cup with the plaster mixture. Before the plaster dries, press small rocks into it all around. Attach two "Y"-shaped sticks to the inside of the cup, to protrude from the top of the well to hold the bucket. Another stick laid in the "Y's" can have a yarn rope with a thimble bucket attached with tape or glue. The little well can be filled and the bucket can really draw water.

Make little clay bowls from the adobe mixture to place near the well and in the houses. Add straw or dried grass to the mixture for thatched roofs. This desert scene can be proudly displayed at home. It makes a wonderful history or geography project for school, too.

## TOY PEOPLE

Your children can make toy people from wooden clothespins. The old-fashioned kind without a spring work best because their shape suggests a head and two long legs. Use pipe cleaners for arms. Glue on bits of fabric or colored tissue paper for clothing. Yarn or cotton is ideal for hair and beards.

## PLAY ANIMALS

Kids love to make little sheep from spools covered with cotton balls. Make small cardboard cylinders for legs and attach them with glue. Youngsters can make other animals with fake fur or felt to cover the spools. Allow these animals to dry completely before the kids play with them.

## PUPPET THEATER

A large box might become a puppet theater for hand puppets. This box should be used upside-down so that the children can work the puppets from under the box. Help youngsters cut the stage opening in one side of the box, leaving a wide frame all around. They can decorate the side of the frame facing the audience. Using colored yarn dipped in glue, the children can coil and twirl it into a pretty design for the stage and write the words "Puppet Theater." They will also want to add the thespian symbols, the smiling and frowning masks.

Encourage a little seamstress to make a curtain for the puppet stage. Show the child how to thread a needle and how to hem two pieces of brightly colored material on both the long edges of each piece. To hang the curtains she can attach a large safety pin to a strong piece of cord and run it through the hem on one long edge of each piece of material. Hang the curtains across the stage opening by attaching the string with strong tape or by punching holes in the sides of the theater box.

## BUILDING FORTS

Save lots of shoe boxes for your child to use as large building blocks to make a child-size fort in which to hide. He can also help you make blocks from clean milk cartons. Just fold the peaked end flat and tape it with strong packaging tape. The child may want to cover these boxes with adhesive-backed paper in a handsome design to match his room, or to look like wood or brick. He will long enjoy using these blocks to build towers (which are not noisy when they crash). Box blocks are also safer for children who throw blocks.

## MAKE AN IGLOO

Your child will adore using sugar cubes to construct a little house for toy people. He can turn a shoe box upside-down and glue the sugar cubes on all sides for a flat-topped house. For an igloo, he can use an inverted whipped topping container.

## DOLLHOUSE

A wonderful dollhouse can be made with four boxes stacked and taped together so that all four openings face the child: two form the upstairs and two are the downstairs. Let the children decorate the walls with pages from a discarded wallpaper book or from old wrapping paper or fabric. Pieces of carpet gleaned from the scrap pile of a new house site are perfect for the floor. Help your child make a braided rug from strips of fabric; or together, weave rugs on a small, child-size loom. You might have bits of the fabrics and carpet used in your own home. Your child will love decorating the dollhouse as a copy of her own home.

## DOLLHOUSE FURNITURE

Tiny furniture is fun to create from trash collectibles. A spool or film can becomes the pedestal for a table. The table-top can be an oatmeal container top, a circle of cardboard, or a coffee can lid. A chair might be fashioned from a small box. A sofa could be some tiny pillows or sponges stacked and glued together, covered with bits of fabric. A postage stamp or sticker could become a wall hanging. Perhaps a matchbox bed will have clothespins for four posters. Little acorn cups can decorate the table. Your children will spend hours decorating their "home."

## PLAYHOUSE BOX

If space permits, get a large appliance box for a garage playhouse. With adults and kids working together, a refrigerator box can become a castle, with carpet roller tubes added as towers. Dad's help will be needed to secure the towers in place with wire. Your child may even want to use papier mâché on the outside for a stone effect and have big brother construct a wooden platform inside (or use a stool) so the child can look out of the top to watch for invaders.

## JUST FOR FUN

Your child will look forward to rainy days as the best ones of the year if you can take a little time to do some creative crafts with her. If you have only a little time to spare, get her started on the craft project and then do your work alongside her. Your nearness communicates companionship and caring. And your periodic encouragement as she creates will stimulate her to continue her endeavors.

If you have an hour or two to spare, you will have as much fun as your son or daughter in making the following projects.

### BEAUTY SHOP

Give your kids fashion magazines and a mirror, comb, and brush. Make a mixture of three tablespoons of sugar dissolved in one cup of warm water. The children can dip the comb into the sugar water and style their own hair just like the fashion models'. Although the sugar water will not harm their hair, and will wash right out, it will make the hair stiff enough to stand up or out in even the weirdest hairdos.

### MAKE-UP TRICKS

Make-up tricks are fun on a rainy day. Give your girls beauty magazines and show them how to follow the make-up tips. This can occupy a down-in-the-dumps teenager happily for hours. A preteen will find it a special treat to be allowed to use all of Mom's make-up. Even little girls would adore being allowed to play with make-up on a rainy day. But supervise the activity to protect your beauty products, walls, and furnishings.

Little boys may want to play movie make-up artists and work on sister's or Mom's face, just for fun. They may also have fun aging themselves as if for a movie. They can try to turn themselves into old men and powder their hair.

What historical figure is your child studying in school? Have the child find a picture of the person in his history book. Give the youngster some make-up and ask him to try to make his face look like the historical figure's. Using his own face as a canvas teaches your child observation and develops his artistic abilities. Show him about contouring, using darker make-up to make certain areas recede and lighter make-up to bring other areas forward or make them appear larger. Your kids may spend all afternoon transforming themselves into famous people. Parents can play "Guess Who."

## STAINED GLASS

To make a "stained glass" window, have your child cut out the centers of two pieces of black construction paper, leaving about three-fourths of an inch black frame all around. Cut two pieces of waxed paper the size of the outer edges of the black paper frames. Lay the frames aside.

The next steps of this project should be supervised and proper safety precautions taken, depending on the age of your child. The youngster should put one piece of waxed paper on the ironing board, which you have protected with a cloth. Onto this wax paper he can scrape lots of shavings from bits of broken wax crayons. (This can be done with a knife, a grater, or with a pencil sharpener.) Use several different colors. Help the child place the second piece of waxed paper on top of the first and iron with a moderately warm iron until the crayons melt and the waxed papers stick together. He can insert this stained glass between the two black window frames and tape or glue them together.

These "stained glass" panels can be used to decorate window openings in a toy house, church, synagogue, or museum, which he can make from a box. Place a flashlight inside the box to illuminate the windows. Or he may instead be delighted to hang the stained glass in the window of his own room.

## SHRINK ART

A project that is especially fun and has unpredictable results is for the kids to shrink plastics in your oven. It is important to do all shrink projects in a well-ventilated area. Open a door or window to prevent fumes from collecting in the kitchen.

Have the child try making monsters by drawing faces with permanent markers on plastic foam cups. Place these on a cookie sheet protected with waxed paper and bake at 325°F. Watch through the oven door and when the melting plastic stops wiggling, remove the pan immediately and set it aside to cool. The melting process can require from a few seconds to two or three minutes, so watch carefully.

Make other interesting shrink crafts by melting plastic strawberry cartons and interspersing them with pretty colored plastic beads. As the creations cool they harden in unusual shapes. These can be strung for wind chimes or mobiles.

Place a foreign coin or other piece of metal inside a clear plastic cup and put it in the oven. After it shrinks and while it is still hot, pierce the plastic with an ice pick or toothpick to make a hole for stringing. This must be done immediately after removing it from the oven. The piece will harden in a couple of minutes and make an attractive key chain or necklace.

Children can draw pictures to shrink by using permanent markers on plastic foam meat trays. Cut out the shapes and bake them. If you want the object to be flat when finished, place another flat pan on top of it immediately after removing it from the oven, or during baking. The colors become much more intense when the art is shrunk.

## "WHATCHAMACALLITS"

Scraps of wood can provide a wonderful occupation for a rainy day. Place the young artist at a surface he cannot damage. A good way to delineate and confine an OK mess area is to use a large scrap of bright carpet. Give him a hammer and nails, if you wish. But for a quieter activity, give him carpenter's glue. He can construct a "whatchamacallit" statue by gluing various sizes and shapes of wooden scraps into a marvelous free-form sculpture that is thought-provoking to all who view it. Color variations can be achieved if different kinds of wood are used. Wood can be sanded smooth either before gluing or after the glue is dried.

"Whatchamacallits" can also be made with plastic foam packing pieces, using either compatible glue or nails. It's easier for small children who haven't learned to nail successfully into wood.

## PICTURE WINDOW

Another good story-telling activity that can occupy your children all day requires a plastic roll-up window shade. Purchase a cheap one and keep it for this special purpose. The oldest child unrolls the shade about two feet and tells the first part of a familiar story, perhaps "Cinderella." As this child tells the story, the other children begin illustrating the tale right on the shade, using felt-tipped markers.

The shade can be unrolled as the story-telling progresses farther and farther so that more and more pictures can be drawn. If *permanent* markers are used the children can color the pictures more elaborately later. The shade can hang in the child's window permanently, or two children can hold and unwind it when the story-telling is repeated. This is an especially good activity when an older child is required to baby-sit younger children.

If the children prefer to draw a new story each time they play, have them use *dry-erase* felt-tipped markers (available at office or teacher supply stores) or washable crayons. Both of these can be erased so that another story can be illustrated later.

## TOTEM POLES

Your child will enjoy making totem poles from wood scraps or from stacked boxes. Give him paints or permanent felt-tipped markers to create a special totem for his room. Several children together might create a large totem for the yard by using big pieces of plastic packing foam and gluing them together. The totem can also be painted with model paint or acrylics, both of which are waterproof, so it can be placed outdoors. The totem can be secured in a can of plaster of paris (available in variety or hardware stores) which dries quickly and provides a stable base. Or you can dig a hole in the ground and pack dirt around the base of the totem.

## CAMP INDOORS

Give your child a cozy corner for quiet indoor "camping." Put up your card table and throw a sheet or blanket over it to make a delightful tent. Little ones will want to take their naps inside. In wintertime, place the "tent" in the room with the fireplace and have a "campfire." Roast hot dogs and marshmallows and sing campfire songs. Give your child his drink in a canteen. If you have no fireplace, make a pretend campfire with sticks placed around a flashlight covered with a red cloth or orange cellophane.

## PLASTER PLAY

A fun craft medium your children can try is plaster of paris, which is available at discount variety, hardware, and craft stores. It is inexpensive, simple to use, and can make a great variety of projects. The only disadvantage I have found is that the projects break easily if dropped, so be careful.

Make plaster castings by adding the powder to water, stirring, and pouring the mixture into any plastic container. A whipped topping carton filled with plaster might yield a little tree stump when unmolded and painted. The children can decorate it with felt leaves, acorns, and a little squirrel on top.

## PLASTER JEWELRY

Plastic lids can be filled with a little layer of plaster (see above) to make a pretty pendant or a sheriff's badge. Spray the lid with nonstick kitchen spray for easy unmolding. Push a safety pin into the surface of the plaster before it sets up. This will be the back of the finished badge. After it is set, unmold it and paint it as desired, scratching a design on it with a nail, if the child wishes.

## HANDPRINT GIFTS

A pie pan makes a good mold to hold a handprint for Grandmother. Be sure to write your child's name and the date before the plaster of paris (see above) dries. Or pour a plaque in any shape. When it is nearly hardened, the child can draw or write on it by scratching the surface with a stick.

## SNOW PEOPLE

Do your youngsters live in a hot climate and never get to see snow? Or do they wish for winter's snowy fun during the summer? Help them to make a huge papier mâché snowman for your yard or their room. This project is lots of fun for a group of children who have patience enough for the week-long creation period.

Mix wallpaper paste according to directions, or use a mixture of half white glue and half water. You can even use flour mixed with enough water to give it a soupy consistency. Tear long strips of newspaper, dip them into the glue mixture, squeeze gently, and wrap them around very large balloons. Completely cover each of three different size balloons with four layers of gluey strips. Cover paper towel rollers with papier mâché for arms, if desired. Allow these papier mâché balls to dry on wax paper for two days in an airy place.

On the third day, stack the balls by gluing them together and using strips of papier mâché tape to hold them in place and to attach the arms for the snowman shape. When the shape is as the children wish their finished product to be, completely cover it with two more layers of papier mâché. But for these last two layers use white paper towels instead of newspaper. It might be advisable to lay the snowman on its back on wax paper for the drying process, unless it seems very sturdy.

When the snowman is thoroughly dry, several days later, kids can paint or glue on features and then give it a good coat of shellac or varnish. When that's dry, they can add a hat, broom, and scarf, or whatever finishing touches they want. The final step is to sing "Frosty the Snowman" together! This is such fun on a hot summer day.

## "FUNGES"

"Funges" are safe and soft blocks. Simply purchase several large assortment bags of inexpensive sponges in pretty colors for your children. They will love stacking them, sorting them by color, building them like blocks, throwing them as a "pillow" fight, stuffing them into clothes for "fat tummies" or "big muscles." Kids will enjoy balancing them on their heads as they walk, throwing them at targets, and taking them to the bathtub to float as little rafts. There is no end to the play that can be had with "funges."

A laundry basket makes a good storage place for them. The children can have basketball practice as they clean up, by throwing the "funges" across the room into the basket. A basketful is a good gift for a big brother or sister when a new baby is born, or a good birthday gift for any preschooler.

## INDOOR PETS

Your children will love making their own stuffed animals on rainy days. Using a double thickness of any soft, washable fabric, cut out a simple animal shape, keeping arms and legs short and fat. Show your child how to zigzag stitch around the shape, with the wrong sides of the fabric pinned together. Clip the curves and corners for smooth turning. Leave an opening for turning the animal right side out. Let your child stuff his new pet with old, clean hosiery cut into short lengths. A throwaway item, the hosiery is safer than bits of foam rubber which can come out and be swallowed or inhaled. Help your child hand sew up the opening. The new stuffed animal is machine washable and dryable, and squeezably soft. Your child can make facial features by gluing on bits of fabric with fabric glue, which will withstand washing. Or he can paint on features with any waterproof permanent marker or acrylic paints. These will not wash out.

## NATURE CRAFTS

Wash and sun dry peach seeds for adorable toy animals your children can make. Add felt ears, tails, arms, and legs. Eyes are the little wiggly plastic ones from variety stores. Whiskers can be made by dipping black thread into glue which will dry clear. Your children can create a menagerie of adorable animals from these. You might want to add a piece of strip magnet to the back, so the animals can decorate the refrigerator or your child's lunch box. Stronger small magnets which are doughnut shaped are available inexpensively from electronics stores.

You can make animal crafts using other seeds or cotton balls, little pebbles, shells, nuts, acorns, plastic foam balls, Ping-Pong balls, powder puffs, ball fringe, jar lids, or bottle caps. My children even formed adorable animals from white bread with the crusts removed. The bread was spread with white glue and then rolled into balls and molded like clay. They harden nicely.

## PAPER DOLLS

Paper dolls are not as popular today as they were when we were children, but your kids will be entertained all day if you introduce them to the wonders you enjoyed as a child. Get a discarded pattern book from a fabric store and keep it for a rainy day. You can also use magazines and catalogues. Your children can select their favorite models in the books, mount them on cardboard, and cut them out. These might be soldiers, policemen, high-fashion movie stars, dating couples, whatever your children decide to cut out. They can make a stand-up prop for each doll, by cutting a slit in the foot of the doll and another in a straight two-inch piece of cardboard. Place the slits together so the cardboard pieces form a cross that will enable the doll to stand.

If you have a large, full-length photograph of your child which you are willing to sacrifice, he will adore making a paper doll of himself, too.

Clothes for the paper dolls can be cut from colored paper. Show the kids how to trace around the edge of the doll so the clothing will fit and how to cut tabs for the garments at shoulders and sides in order to hang them on the paper doll. Help design a two-sided dress by folding paper in half and cutting out the double dress, leaving the shoulder fold uncut. A slit for the head is all that is needed.

## PRETTY CARDS

Magazines and catalogues provide excellent rainy day entertainment. Children can cut out pictures to make greeting cards and posters, and to frame for room decorations. A toy catalogue can help your child write a "Dear Santa" letter in pictures, even in the middle of the summer! This is a good way to write thank you notes too: "Thank you for my . . ." and the child attaches a catalogue picture of his gift.

## "ME PUPPETS"

What better rainy day fun could your child find than to make a life-sized "Me Puppet"? Poster paper works well for this project, or you can use pieces of cardboard from large boxes. Corrugated cardboard is not recommended because it is too difficult to cut.

Have one child lie down on a large piece of cardboard. Have another person draw all around him. If two pieces of poster paper are used, make sure the separation is at a joint. Cut out the figure of the child and cut off legs and arms at each joint. Make holes at these joints and re-attach the limbs with inexpensive metal brads, purchased at a stationery or variety store.

Have the child draw his face and color his hair on the "Me Puppet." Dress the figure in the child's own clothes. Add a string to the puppet's head and tie it to a yardstick. Now the child stands on a chair and dangles his own life-size "Me Puppet," making it dance and jiggle.

You can add a teaching aspect to this "Me Puppet" by having the child make the puppet do things it is not supposed to do (like fussing at bedtime or throwing a tantrum) and then having the child teach the puppet the proper behavior.

## PANTRY CRAFTS

There are many food items your child can enjoy using in creative play. These are good activities when boredom is brewing or when a whiney or sick child does not seem to be interested in anything. The nice part about these craft activities is that if the child loses interest in or is dissatisfied with his creations, he can eat them. The advantage of these crafts for the parent is that you will usually have on hand the items needed in this section, so you can suggest these play ideas when you don't have time to go to the store to purchase items needed for other types of projects.

### VEGGIE PEOPLE

Let your child try a real potato for making a funny little man. Use toothpick pieces to attach raisin eyes, a carrot nose, a radish mouth, squash ears, etc.

### PEANUT FAMILIES

Little peanut people are fun. Using whole, unshelled peanuts, the child can insert a wire for feet and arms, putting a large raisin or a Cheerio on the ends of each wire for hands and feet. Or draw hands and feet on cardboard or felt and attach with glue. Children will love making entire families of peanut people and making matchbox houses for them.

## CRACKER CONSTRUCTION

Give your child a box of cheese crackers and some toothpicks. Tell him to construct the most elaborate thing he can make by inserting the toothpicks in the holes in the crackers and using them as a construction set.

## MARSHMALLOW SNOWMEN

Marshmallows on a humid day can be marvelous for shaping into snowmen, knights, Santa Claus, dolls, or other imaginary characters. Kids can easily cut them with scissors into desired shapes. Cut marshmallows will stick together if dipped in water. Toothpicks make good legs for little marshmallow animals. Features can be painted on by dipping a toothpick into food coloring.

## PLAY CLAY

Everyone loves the feel of squishy clay or soft dough. You will enjoy working with this medium along with your children. The recipe I find the simplest to make, the most successful to model, and the longest-lasting when placed in airtight storage, is this:

> *3 cups flour*
> *1½ cups salt*
> *1½ tablespoons cream of tartar*
> *3 cups water*
> *3 tablespoons cooking oil*

Stir the ingredients together in a large pot and cook for a couple of minutes on medium high. Turn out onto waxed paper. When it is cool enough to handle, divide the dough into six balls, on six separate pieces of waxed paper. The children will have as much fun finishing the play-clay preparation from this point as they will have playing with it later.

Make a thumb-size impression in each ball and pour into it a good squirt of food coloring; the more coloring, the deeper the color of the finished clay. To each ball add a different, edible scent. You can use lemon extract, vanilla, cinnamon, and peppermint. Of course, this clay does not taste good, so don't recommend eating it; however, if your youngsters are curious enough to taste it, it won't harm them.

Now have the children knead and squeeze the balls until the color is uniform throughout. Store each ball in a separate zipper plastic bag. If clay creations are left in the air, they will dry very hard in a few days and will break if dropped.

---

A word of caution: the dough is easily ground into carpets and is nearly impossible to remove. Use it only where there is a hard-surfaced floor.

---

### BREAD PLAY

Another recipe children enjoy making is a simple bread-dough recipe. It is wonderful for making Christmas tree ornaments, little fruits and vegetables for a playhouse, plaques for the wall, decorations for packages, pendants to wear, or weaving into baskets. The recipe is simple:

*1½ cups salt*
*4 cups sifted flour*
*1¾ cups very hot water*

Knead the dough for ten minutes before rolling. Tell the kids that kneading makes big muscles. Divide the dough into four balls and work with one at a time, storing the others in a plastic bag to keep them from drying out.

Children can roll the dough and cut it with cookie cutters, or shape it with their hands. Long "snakes" of the dough can be flattened and woven into a pretty basket to display fruit or to serve snacks. If you want the dough to brown, brush it with egg white before baking. Normally, it will remain cream colored.

Flour a hard, smooth surface. Roll out the dough to the thickness of your cookie cutters. Flour the cutters and use toothpicks to begin separating the cookie from the cutter. If the cutter has a hole below the handle, blow to help the ornament out. Spray the cookie sheets with nonstick spray. The recipe makes two large panfuls. Save all the scraps for one final rolling out. The ornaments can be placed closely together on the pan, as they do not swell.

Before baking, prepare cookies for hanging by making a hole with a drinking straw. The hole will shrink to a smaller size during baking. Press dough through a garlic press to make hair for animal or people shapes. Use a toothpick or knife to carve faces or to add any desired features.

You can color the ornaments in several ways. You might want to color the dough with food coloring mixed uniformly throughout. Using a paint brush or cotton swab, you can also paint the ornaments with straight food color before baking. This is an excellent method if you want the color on only one side. For ornaments painted on both sides, you must paint after baking is complete. Use acrylic paints.

Bake the ornaments at 200°F. for four hours or more, depending on their thickness. They should be completely hard when you test them with your fingernail. To prevent cracking, allow them to cool thoroughly in the oven. Whether or not you paint the finished products, you must seal them with clear spray sealer on *all* surfaces in order to prevent moisture or insects from ruining them. These decorations are sturdy and will last indefinitely.

## GINGERBREAD MAN

Children will enjoy acting out favorite stories on a rainy day. Many suggestions for this play are in the chapter "If I Were You." One suggestion that is really rainy day special is to make a giant gingerbread cookie together.

SIFT:  *5 cups flour*
*1½ teaspoons baking soda*
*½ teaspoon salt*
*2 teaspoons ginger*
*2 teaspoons cinnamon*
*1 teaspoon cloves*

CREAM: *1 cup sugar*
*1 cup shortening*
*1 egg*
*1 cup molasses*
*2 teaspoons vinegar*

Add the dry ingredients and stir together. Have your children form the dough into three balls and chill them at least an hour. While you are waiting for the dough to chill, read the children the story of "The Gingerbread Man."

When the dough is ready, use a greased cookie sheet. The children can place one of the balls at the top of the cookie sheet to become the head of the gingerbread man. With their hands they can press the dough ball flat to about one-third-inch thickness.

Show the kids how to roll the next ball between their palms until a "snake" is formed. This is placed beneath the head to form the arms. Position them in any desired way, perhaps with one arm waving. The kids can pat the "snake" to flatten the dough and to connect it securely to the head.

The third ball is also made into a "snake" and placed on the cookie sheet beneath the head and arms in an upside down "V" to make the legs. Twist the ends to form running feet. Flatten the dough legs to the proper thickness and connect the top of the "V" securely to the arms, forming the body area also.

The children should decorate the little man with raisins and red hots or chocolate drops before baking. Bake at 350° F. for about 30 minutes. Test with your finger to be sure it is not getting too hard for the children to enjoy eating it.

Place the cookie in the oven to bake without telling your children that you are acting out the story of "The Gingerbread Man." Send your children off to play in another room, telling them to listen for the stove buzzer.

Then set the buzzer for fifteen minutes *longer* than necessary for baking. After the *proper* cooking time (before the buzzer rings), remove the cookie from the oven without telling your children. Hide the little ginger man in a fairly difficult place, turn the oven off, and place the empty cookie sheet inside. When the buzzer rings and the children peer into the empty oven, exclaim, "Oh! We must have made a real Gingerbread Man. He ran away!" Sing the little tune, "Run, run as fast as you can. You can't catch me. I'm the Gingerbread Man," as you lead the children on a round-the-house search for the missing little man.

If you teach school, this activity is a good one to do on the first day of classes. As the children search for the Gingerbread Man, they become familiar with the layout of the school or classroom. You might even have the search continue for a day or two to encourage reluctant students to return to class. Of course, when the cookie is found, some child may have conjured up a real little being and will refuse to eat it!

## GAMES TO MAKE AND PLAY

The games you will find in this section are homemade versions of familiar old standbys. Of course, you could buy these games, or you may already have them in a closet or cabinet. But for long hours of delight on a rainy day, your children will get more satisfaction by making their own, and the play will last a lot longer, since part of the fun is in making the game.

### MATCHING SQUARES

Find a friend who will give you an old copy of a magazine you already have. With two identical magazines, your children can make interesting card games. To make a game similar to lotto the child uses one magazine and selects six pictures to mount on one piece of cardboard for each person's individual game board. From the other magazine the child cuts out pictures that match each of the pictures mounted on the players' boards. These individual pictures are turned face down and scrambled. The players draw in turn from the stack of single cards until one player has matched all the pictures on his board. He is the winner. After the boards are exchanged and the pictures rescrambled, the game begins again.

### OLD MAIDS

You can help your child make sturdy playing cards for games like "Old Maids" by cutting out the same pictures from two identical magazines or catalogues. The child can then mount each picture on a separate piece of cardboard. In "Old Maids" the child with the greatest number of matching pairs wins. The losing player should be left holding one odd card, so remember to cut out a picture without matching it to allot for the "old maid" card.

## CONCENTRATION

Matching cards from the game above can also be used for playing "Concentration." Lay all the shuffled cards singly, face down. Each child turns up a card and then tries to turn up its mate. If he fails to turn up a matched pair, the cards must be turned face down again. Whenever he turns up a matched pair, he gets to keep it. The children must remember where the various cards are in order to get matched pairs and win the game.

## CHECKERS

Your children can also make a checkers game on a rainy day. Give them scraps of red and black felt or construction paper to cut into squares and mount on a folded piece of cardboard, 12 inches by 12 inches. Or use felt strips or ribbons 1 inch wide and 12 inches long to weave a checkerboard. For playing pieces, one child can use bottle caps and another, pennies. Any household item will work for playing pieces, even circles of colored paper, as long as the two players can distinguish their own playing pieces.

## TIDDLYWINKS

The game of "tiddlywinks" can be improvised by using coins and any small plastic dish to catch them. Players go one at a time, trying to pop five dimes into the dish from a prescribed distance. To play the game the dimes are dropped on a hard surface floor or counter behind the playing line. (Don't play this on a wood table because the surface could be scratched.) A quarter is laid on the edge of one dime and then sharply snapped onto the floor or counter surface, causing the dime to jump into the air, hopefully in the direction of the dish. The player who gets the most dimes into the dish in five attempts wins.

## TOSS THE BUTTON

For a safe form of darts, play "Toss the Button." Lay a large calendar on the floor. Then mark a line on the floor with masking tape. The children stand behind the line and attempt to toss five buttons onto the daily squares of the calendar. The score is the addition of the calendar numbers on which the buttons land.

Tossing games can take almost any form you and your child can imagine using things at hand. Try tossing dried lentils or nuts into a bowl. Or throw canning jar rings onto a broom handle.

## PICK UP STICKS

Use plastic drinking straws or toothpicks to play an old-fashioned game of "Pick Up Sticks." The child holds a handful of the straws and drops them. The object is to pick up as many as possible without any other straw moving even a tiny bit. Other players watch carefully to be sure the other straws do not move.

## BIG SLURP

Give your child an unsectioned paper plate to make a cute little funny face. He can paint it, glue on yarn hair, and cut a large circle for the mouth. Attach a string about twelve feet long to the back of the plate and pull it through the mouth. Now the little man can be called "Big Slurp" or the "Spaghetti-Eating Man." Hang him on the wall where the game is to be played. Let each child, in turn, pull the string out of his mouth to measure the place she is supposed to stand to throw a bean bag or ball into his mouth.

## PEA SHOOTER

Make a safe pea shooter by using drinking straws with a bit of foil wrapped over the end. Blow through the straw and aim a paper dart at anyone or at a target, perhaps a stuffed animal, or at Big Slurp (see above).

## PUZZLE ME

Have each child make a "Me Puzzle" (as suggested in the "Hooking the New Reader" chapter). Scramble all the puzzles together. Part of the fun is for each child to identify parts of himself as the kids have a contest to see who can work his "Me Puzzle" first.

# HOOKING THE NEW READER

**P**reparing your child to read begins long before you would think it does. Did you know that crawling is an important basic skill which affects his later reading abilities? Your child's motor (muscle) development as a preschooler helps determine his later abilities in more advanced developmental processes.

Children are not born with motor skills. These are developed by stages. A child who sits and watches TV most of the day does not develop his muscles to their best potential. This chapter will help you discover activities that develop your preschool child physically and stimulate his reading-readiness.

Children must learn to measure space by moving their bodies through space. The motion serves as a basis for learning time and energy and spatial concepts and for strengthening large and small muscles, hand-eye coordination, and visual discrimination. All of these abilities are basic to reading. The child learns by situations in play or games which require him to sort out his motor system and develop his skills.

These activities will help the older child who has experienced reading difficulties to correct the problems. Children who have trouble distinguishing "b" from "d" or "was" from "saw" in the early grades are experiencing visual perception problems that could be caused by faulty spatial concepts, poor coordination, and poor sense of body awareness!

A child must learn to maintain balance in order to develop a vertical reference or spatial concept of "up and down," "in front of," and "behind." These concepts lead to distinguishing sides of the body and to differentiation between "left and right," between "back and forth." This internal awareness is called "laterality," and until it is developed the child cannot develop a sense of direction in space.

Basic reading ability requires control of the eyes. Reading requires the eyes to sweep from left to right and back again in a smooth, rhythmic pattern. That return sweep is very quick with no visual cues for guidance, and must remain rhythmic and accurate for good reading progress. Comprehension is believed to be influenced by this rhythmic sequence.

The activities you will discover in this chapter are simple to do, and most of the equipment required is already available in your home. You can initiate many of these activities on the spur of the moment, wherever you are, and they are all fun for the whole family. Following the ideas here will develop family habits that will create a lifetime of reading enjoyment.

## BALANCE AND LARGE MUSCLE DEVELOPMENT

These are beginning skills for your youngster. You will enjoy watching him progress as you do these activities together. He will take pride in each successful attempt and will be inspired to attempt more and more as he sees your delight in his growth.

### UP WE GO

Climbing is a wonderful developer of large muscles. Use stairs as a learning tool. Help your toddler to go up and down successfully. Hold his hand and practice repeatedly with him, encouraging him, by age three, to alternate feet, using right-left-right-left, as he ascends and descends. This takes lots of practice, and should be mastered by age four. Teach him to be careful, but not fearful.

If you have no stairs in your home, you can help your toddler develop these muscles by repeatedly going up and down one porch step, or use a low, sturdy stool, or a stack of large books. Make it a game to practice the left-right foot alternation on any stairs you encounter in public places.


## LOOK AT ME

Preschoolers naturally enjoy jumping, hopping, skipping, galloping, climbing, running. If you go outside with your child often, and watch as she does these natural antics, you can compliment her accomplishments and show her how to do other movements. A child likes to perform for loving adults. You will be teaching her how to play freely outside, an important thing for any child to learn.


## WALKING THE LINE

A walking board or balance beam teaches laterality, visual perception, balance, and rhythm. Encourage the child to do these activities on a low wall, a railroad tie, several cement blocks placed end to end, or on a professional balance beam from a gymnastics supply company (depending on your budget and space).

He can practice walking across without falling. Next suggest walking with a weight (a can of vegetables, perhaps). Have him walk across the beam, changing the weight from hand to hand. He can walk with a chalkboard eraser or a sponge on his head; or walk and throw a bean bag at a target on command. He can walk across the beam while bouncing a ball or walk sideways or backward. He can also go to the center, kneel, straighten one leg, stand and go to the end, or skip or hop.

Have fun by doing the activities with your child. Make mistakes yourself to let your child know that it's OK to falter. As his skills develop, have contests with family members, or let the child perform his skills for an audience of friends. These are activities that can begin as soon as your child can walk steadily and then progress in difficulty as your child grows older and more skilled.

## FOLLOW THE LEADER

Follow-the-leader activities teach a child to judge space between himself and others and to learn control of his muscles. The leader can do various motor activities such as carrying weights; balancing a magazine on his head; varying the size of his stride; galloping; leading with the right, then the left foot; skipping; hopping on the left, then the right foot; going backward or sideways; jumping on spots. These are just a few ideas. You and your youngsters will think of many more.

## ROCK-A-BYE

A rocking seat teaches balance and visual perception. Children can practice pure balance on a "seesaw" by standing in the middle and moving back and forth, experimenting with the distribution of their weight.

You and your child can construct a simple balance toy by cutting the rockers from an old rocking chair. Attach a low wooden platform between the rockers. Your child can use this wooden rocker toy to practice, in sitting position, for perfect balance and then with back and forth and sideways movements. In standing position he can experiment with his feet in various positions. As he is rocking back and forth have him throw and catch soft objects like a bean bag. Tell him to move his arms and feel the effects.

## CHALKING UP BIG MUSCLES

A large chalkboard is an excellent learning tool in the home and will give more hours of play than almost any other item. Commercial ones are very expensive, but you can make one easily and with little expense.

Purchase a half sheet of Masonite and mount it on a wall in your child's play area. Paint the smooth surface of the Masonite with several coats of chalkboard paint in a color to match the room. Make a chalk trough by adding a suitable piece of molding. Your children will write and draw on this for years. To encourage large muscle development, the pictures drawn with the chalk should be big.

Give preschoolers only fat crayons, large pieces of paper, large paintbrushes, fat pencils, and block erasers. These tools develop the larger muscles of the hand, which *must* be strengthened before the smaller muscles, or your child will be inadequately prepared for writing and thus hindered when he reaches kindergarten. The rule is: "The smaller the child, the larger the tool or toy."

## AROUND THE BLOCK

Indoors, one of the best toys for gross motor development is a set of good building blocks. The sets of plain, large blocks, designed with arches, semi-circles, and triangles to fit into each other and to fit perfectly into their own box, are among the best toy investments you can make. Your children will enjoy these from toddler to teenager.

If you cannot afford to purchase these blocks, do not buy a smaller set. You can make a set of blocks for free, if you are willing to spend the time. At building sites, cabinet shops, and lumber yards blocks of wood are thrown away every day. Make a request for these. Measure the sizes and shapes of the commercial blocks used in schools and kindergartens, at teaching supply centers, and in toy stores. Find a carpenter friend who will cut the wood scraps to the right size for you. Someone who has professional tools can cut an entire set in a few minutes.

If you have access to an electric sander, use it on all the blocks first. Then, each evening when you are relaxing in front of the TV, fine-sandpaper a few blocks, until the set is complete.

These store well in a grapefruit box or a box used to ship poultry to chicken restaurants. (This type of waxed, sturdy box with hand holes is great for all kinds of toy storage. Be sure to clean the box first with a good disinfectant. I have always used isopropyl alcohol or chlorine bleach because neither requires much rinsing. Dry the box in the sun for a day.)

Making blocks would be an excellent project for an expectant family to do while waiting the nine months for a new baby. By the time a child reaches school age he feels he is "too big" for ABC blocks, but he never outgrows the joy of construction with these sturdy, plain ones.

## CLAY PLAY

Another excellent activity for preschoolers to develop large muscles is to play with clay. Go to a ceramic shop and purchase several pounds of commercial clay in a large plastic bag. This can be used and reused for months or even years, if the bag is kept airtight, and it is less expensive and more versatile than the typical clay sold for children in toy departments. If the clay begins to dry out or get crumbly, add a little water to the bag and seal it for a few days.

If your child makes something he really wants to keep, you can air dry it and keep it on a shelf, as it will be too fragile to use for play. If you wish the object to be more durable, have it fired in a kiln at the ceramic shop so your child can take pride in it for years. The firing process turns the clay into ceramic.

Just for fun, look for clay by a riverbed. Ask a local potter to suggest the best area to dig clay. You can collect it for free.

## HAND-EYE COORDINATION AND VISUAL DISCRIMINATION

Did you know that when you play "catch" or work a puzzle with your youngster you are helping him to develop his reading and writing abilities? Coordinating the hand movement with the eyes is basic to writing. And visual discrimination is necessary for distinguishing letters and words. Read on to learn other activities that are fun and incorporate learning skills.

## MAKE IT FOR FUN

Your children will have fun making their own bean bags. For a simple rectangular-shaped one, help your youngster sew a small "pillowcase" shape (about six inches by four inches) on three sides. Fill it with dried lentils, and stitch the remaining side closed.

## ANIMAL BEAN BAGS

Animal-shaped bean bags are easy to make. Your child can trace the outline of any animal from a coloring book onto a piece of plain paper. It should be a simple shape with fat legs, for ease in stuffing the bean bag. When she cuts out the paper pattern, she can pin it to a double thickness of fabric. When cutting the fabric, have her cut about one-half inch outside the pattern edges, to allow for stitching. I recommend vinyl material for its wipe-clean advantage. However, any double-knit or non-raveling fabric will do.

With wrong sides together, help your child machine or hand stitch the two pieces of fabric together, leaving one end open about three inches. Turn the bag inside-out and fill with dried lentils, uncooked rice, or soybeans. Stitch the end closed.

If your child cannot find or draw a suitable animal shape, simply make a rectangular or oval bean bag. When it is complete, sew on four slightly-stuffed rectangles or ovals for legs and a stuffed circle for the head. She can add ears, facial features, and tail by gluing on pieces of felt.

## JUGGLING

Your child could make an entire circus of animal bean bags (see instructions above) and use them to practice juggling.

## TARGETS

It is a challenge to devise different targets for bean bags or balls. Targets can be as simple as an old mailbox, bucket, or coffee can, or as elaborate as your children wish to make them. Perhaps a large cardboard box painted to look like a pet store would be a good target for animal bean bags. (See above instructions for making animal bean bags.) Help your child cut holes for windows and doors. Then have contests to see who can get the most animals into the pet store.

## PLAYING CATCH

A bean bag or ball can aid in the development of your
child's judgment, visual perception, and coordination of the
large muscles. Begin by throwing one bean bag back and
forth to your child, then change distances. Throw two bags of
equal weight back and forth simultaneously. Throw high and
low. Have him catch with his left or right hand, on call. Have
him throw the bean bag or ball at a target or series of
different targets; then try for the targets blindfolded. Have
him practice juggling several bean bags or balls. All these fun
activities are teaching your child hand-eye coordination as
well as giving him special time with you. Note that these are
also good activities for older siblings to do with younger
ones, as it is sometimes difficult to find activities children of
widely differing ages will all enjoy.

## PUZZLES

Working puzzles promotes visual discrimination, a vital
prereading skill that helps a child later learn to identify the
different shapes of the various letters. At each stage of your
child's development provide him with puzzles and toys appropriate for his age, from baby to teenager. Work puzzles
together with young children to help them learn how to do
them and with older children for family fun and relaxed
communication.

---

As you and your child make selections, remember that any
toy too advanced will discourage the child and cause tan-
trums. One too babyish will bore him. Ages recommended
by toy manufacturers are generally an accurate guide.

---

## ME PUZZLE

By age four a child will adore a puzzle of himself. Select
a large photograph which you have in duplicate, or have an
inexpensive photograph taken in a variety store, specifically
for the purpose of puzzle making. Using rubber cement or
photographic adhesive, help the child to glue the photo on

sturdy cardboard and allow it to dry overnight. (Any type of glue will work, but the ones recommended will not ripple the photo.)

On the cardboard side, the child can draw a series of large shapes and cut them out. You may need to help if the cardboard is thick. This puzzle will be worked and reworked through the years. It also makes a good birthday present to give to a cousin or best friend. Find a small box for storage of the puzzle, and mount the duplicate photo on the lid.

## PUZZLE BOARDS

Older children who enjoy jigsaw puzzles will find a puzzle board much more satisfactory than a table because, if the puzzle is not completed at one sitting (and they almost never are), you can store it undisturbed under the bed until next play time.

Help your children make a good puzzle lapboard, which is great for studying, drawing, feeding a sick child, and many other uses. Have a lumberyard or your teenagers cut a piece of Masonite for you in a size about 18 by 24 inches, rounding all the corners. In the center of one of the long sides have them cut out a semicircle so the board fits around the child's stomach area when seated in a chair or bed. The kids can sand any rough edges and paint or decorate the lapboard with decals or their initials, if they wish. Seal with clear sealer.

## TACTILE SENSES REINFORCE LEARNING

"Touchy-feely" things are great for helping a child remember new learning experiences. Below you will find a number of ideas to use your child's tactile senses to reinforce recognizing letters and numbers.

### A LEARNING FEELING

A novel way for your child to learn the alphabet is with a tray of cornmeal or raw oatmeal. She will enjoy the feeling as she makes letters and words with her fingers in the dry meal. The tactile senses which are stimulated will help her remember the shapes of the letters.

## BIG LETTERS OUTSIDE

In the sandbox outside, on the beach, in the dry dirt of an empty lot, or in the squishy mud after a rain, encourage the child to write with his fingers or toes. Kids can also do this for a short while in fresh snow, but take precautions to avoid frostbite. The benefits of such play are many: making large letters develops large muscles; tactile senses are stimulated to reinforce learning; repetition improves memory; fun makes learning enjoyable! Your child will never forget making his name in letters larger than himself on a wet seashore.

## EMERY BOARD ALPHABET

When you find emery boards on sale, purchase several packages to make a wonderful set of letters for learning. Make block letters by gluing the emery boards onto large, unlined index cards. Have your youngster trace each letter with his fingers as he names it. As he grows, have him play a game of feeling the letter with his eyes closed and identifying it.

## TEXTURED LETTERS

You can also make "feely" alphabet cards from other textures. Cut large block letters from velvet, fake fur, oilcloth, or sandpaper. Mount each letter on individual index cards. You can also make raised letters by writing on colored paper with a thick line of white glue. Allow this to dry overnight and the hardened glue will make raised letters. For an older child who already knows the alphabet, use the glue to add dots and dashes beneath each letter for Morse code. Or add dot patterns for Braille letters, which are shown in your encyclopedia. Learning these other ways of writing increases your child's awareness of others and his ability to communicate with all people.

This is a wonderful teaching tool for visually handicapped children.

# DEVELOPING SMALL MOTOR SKILLS

Activities which may not seem to relate to reading readiness will develop small muscles in the hand to prepare a child for writing. Reserve these activities until the child is four or older and has already performed many activities listed earlier in this chapter to promote good development of larger muscles.

## USING SCISSORS

> The scissors activities which follow should be used progressively, adding each subsequent activity only after the child has thoroughly mastered the previous one.

Cutting with scissors is an important skill. Get a good pair of child-size, blunt metal scissors to begin cutting. If the child seems to be left-handed, by all means, equip your home with "lefty" scissors. If you think that is unimportant, try to cut something with your right-handed scissors held in your left hand; it is almost impossible.

> A child, by age four, is still somewhat ambidextrous, but observe which hand seems to gain preference. Never force a child to change his "handedness."

Teach safety from the first time a child uses scissors, even though he is beginning with blunt ones. Teach him which things are appropriate to cut and which are not. When first learning any skill it is just as easy to learn good habits as it is to learn bad ones. By demonstration show him that some scissors are for paper, some for metal, and some for fabric. Teach him that scissors should never be used on the wrong materials. Practice handing the child scissors and taking them back in a safe manner, with the handle pointed toward the receiver. Teach him to sit or walk slowly when using scissors, never to run or climb.

## MAKE CONFETTI

To begin with scissor cutting, give your child a piece of paper, not too thick, and ask how many pieces he can snip from it. Give him a box or tray to catch the pieces as they fall. These can be saved for confetti or for collage art. Use old newspapers, magazines, catalogues, or junk mail.

## CUTTING LINES

After your child is comfortable with the use of scissors and can simply cut paper with ease (see above), the next stage is to teach your child to cut on a line. Draw one straight line on a paper with a felt-tipped pen, so that the mark is thick, and ask your child to cut along the line. When he has mastered this, draw a zig-zag line.

## CUTTING SQUIGGLES

When he can cut confidently, tell him he is now ready to make "squiggles." These are fun, but you will have to draw the first ones for him. Cut a large circle from paper. Use a felt-tipped marker or crayon and begin at one edge, drawing a line that spirals inward. Each line within the spiral should be about three-fourths of an inch from the one outside it, ending with a large dot in the center. Help your child begin at the outer edge of the circle and cut along the line until he reaches the dot. The resulting "squiggle" will bounce up and down as he suspends it by holding the center dot. You can make "squiggles" from squares, rectangles, and triangles, and in many colors of paper. These are fun to hang as a mobile by tying them to yarn on a wire coathanger.

## CUTTING FIGURES

Only after learning to cut with ease any simple lines drawn on paper should the child be encouraged to cut out forms from coloring books, magazines, etc. As he progresses to cutting out more intricate shapes, you may want to give him fingernail scissors or small embroidery scissors, so that small details can be cut more easily.

## CUTTING FABRIC

After mastering paper cutting, you will want to allow your child to try cutting fabric with fabric scissors. As these are pointed and much sharper the child must be a little older, more experienced with scissors, and supervised.

## PAPER PLAY

Cutting is an important skill that teaches finger dexterity as well as hand-eye coordination. Tearing paper also develops small muscles and teaches another skill—pulling the paper two different ways at the same time. This can be a difficult skill for youngsters at first. Have him practice with paper towels or cheap paper napkins and junk mail.

## SNOWFLAKES

When your child has mastered cutting and tearing, show him the magic of paper snowflakes. The first snowflakes can be made from a piece of paper folded in half two ways (so that if the paper were unfolded the folds would make the shape of a cross.) Keeping the paper folded, the child cuts or tears the resulting four corners. By unfolding the paper, she will delight in the snowflake she has made.

Of course, the more times she folds and cuts the paper, the fancier the snowflake, but also the greater thickness she must cut or tear. Use thin, cheap paper napkins or onion-skin typing paper. Help her mount her snowflakes on colored paper to show the pattern more brilliantly.

Children love to hang these snowflakes all around their room and on their windows in winter. Remember the fun activity again in mid-summer!

## 52 PICK-UP

Another skill for small-muscle development is picking up small objects. Have the children "rain" pennies, unpopped corn, or playing cards, then pick them up. The game rules are that the child can use both hands but pick up only one item at a time. Give a simple prize for the child who picks up the most. This may seem like a silly game, but the child is learning finger dexterity. You can also use it to teach principles of picking up whatever is spilled onto the floor.

## ENCOURAGE CONSTRUCTION PLAY

Construction toys suitable for your child's age help strengthen small muscles and promote hand-eye coordination. And the child who builds repeatedly with construction toys certainly nurtures his creative abilities.

## HOLE PUNCHING

Punching holes in paper with a hole punch is fun for youngsters. Children can make great confetti by collecting the holes in a box. The hole punch helps develop the small muscles of the hands. Encourage the child to punch with both left and right hands, to develop both. If the confetti makes a mess, give the child the vacuum cleaner for more fun. To the child vacuuming can become a game, not work, as it is to you. The child may become so fascinated with watching the paper being sucked away that he may delight in vacuuming as a regular chore.

## COLORING BOOKS

Give your children coloring books and help them learn to color within the lines. As your little ones color, do not worry that by doing so they are thwarting their own creativity and self-expression, as artists will tell you. Encourage your children to take pride in keeping within the lines of the book as they color. But remind yourself, this is not an art lesson. This is a lesson in hand-eye coordination and development of the small muscles in your child's hand. Both of these skills are vital before your child can master verbal skills in writing and reading.

## PREPARATORY READING ACTIVITIES

In the section that follows you will discover many ideas for family fun that will teach your children about words. The young child just beginning to want to learn to read is fascinated with letters and words. Each new skill he masters is a source of great pride and the foundation for his future attitude about reading and learning. Be careful that you share and encourage his enthusiasm so that he never loses it.

Obviously, you would not do all these word activities at one time. With preschoolers, spend days or weeks on each activity, until your child thoroughly understands the concept that is being taught. Then move on to the next stage. With older children, many of these ideas can reinforce learning in school or help the child grasp a concept with which he is having difficulty.

## LEARNING LETTERS

A toy that is worth the investment and prepares your child for reading is a set of magnetic letters. Keep these on your refrigerator or washing machine, or in your office or workroom, so that while you work you can teach your youngster as she plays nearby.

If you find it handier to have the letters in something which the child can take from room to room, store them in a flat-topped metal lunchbox. The letters will adhere to the top of the box. It is better if you paint the box a solid color because figures or designs which usually decorate these lunch boxes will detract your child from concentrating on the letters.

If you cannot afford a new set of letters, find someone whose children have outgrown them, and purchase the set at garage-sale prices. Two sets are worthwhile because the kids can write more words.

## LEARNING VOWELS

After your child can identify letters, teach her that the most useful ones are the vowels. It is easier for her to remember them if you play this little game: Place the vowels in a row on the refrigerator, removing the other letters. Tell her to give you the "E." Take it away, leading the child to the next room. Say, "I borrowed your 'E.' Now I owe you an 'E.'" Repeat this several times until she understands the concept of "owing." Now shorten and sing-song the sentence, "I, O, U, A, E." Have the child sing-song this a few times before returning the "E." Now she knows her vowels! Have her arrange the vowels to read the sing-song she has just chanted.

## USING VOWELS

Explain that with vowels in the middle, the child can use other letters as partners on each side to make words. Demonstrate with several three-letter words which use each of the different vowels in the middle.

## RHYME TIME

Play a game teaching the concept of rhymes. Say a three-letter word and help the child to spell it with magnetic letters. Ask her to tell you as many words as she can to rhyme with the word she formed. Each time she thinks of a new rhyme have her change the beginning consonant accordingly to make the new word.

This game can also be done with a pencil and paper, if you have no magnetic letters. Or cut out large letters individually from magazines to make the alphabet. You can also print each large letter on separate index cards.

## CREATING WORDS

Show the child how to keep the beginning consonant and the vowel and change the ending consonants to make many new words.

## LIST NEW WORDS

A child in kindergarten will enjoy copying the words she makes with magnetic letters onto a piece of paper to keep a record of how many words she can read.

For example, she can make a sheet of "at" words. Show her how to go through the alphabet to find as many "at" words as possible: *a*t, *b*at, *c*at (skip over "eat" because it doesn't rhyme and will confuse the child at this stage), *f*at, *h*at, etc.

## WORD-A-DAY

Other skills can help make reading fun. Your child's vocabulary is important for making reading easier and more pleasurable. Form a family "word-a-day" habit. You might purchase a calendar designed to teach a new word each day. The cost amounts to a few cents a day and is a good investment. If you cannot afford this, assign each member of the family one day of the week to look up a new word to teach to other family members. He should give the spelling and definition, and use the word in several sentences.

Keep a list of the new words. At the end of each month have a contest to see which child can define and use correctly the most words of the month. Award a prize.

## GOOD GRAMMAR

Language skills are so important. If you know you speak incorrectly, get a grammar book and force yourself to learn the rules and follow them. Children learn more by imitation than any other way. If your child makes some mistakes frequently, correct them gently. Do not fail to teach your child correctness because his mistakes are "cute." He may be very embarrassed in adulthood to learn that something he has been saying all his life is not correct.

## NAME THAT PLACE

For beginning readers, print the names of everyday objects and hang them around the house. For instance, in your child's room have signs that say, "wall," "door," "window," etc. You might want to read and practice the words with the child frequently. Or you may do this with preschoolers and not even call attention to the signs. A few weeks later, write the word on a piece of paper and ask the child if he can read it. You will be amazed at how often he has made the connection and remembered the way the word looks. Children learn by observation.

For children studying a foreign language this is also a great help for learning vocabulary words. Have them print and hang their own word signs because in doing so the spelling is impressed on their minds.

## ALPHABET NOODLES

Give the youngster uncooked alphabet noodles and ask him to copy the words which you print, or copy words from a magazine, by gluing the noodles onto paper. This activity is good for making Christmas cards, Valentines, birthday greetings, get well cards, and for making a note to Grandfather.

## BUILDING VERBAL SKILLS

As your child gets into school there are many activities you can do with him at home that will make learning fun and augment his skills with words, thereby improving his grades in reading, language, spelling, writing, and all verbal skills. You will have fun doing these activities as a family, and every member will benefit from them.

## ALL-AROUND FUN

As you drive around town, repeat little verses that are language aids. Examples are: "*I* before *E*, except after *C*, or when sounding like *A*, as in *neighbor* and *weigh*." And, "An *E* on the end makes the vowel in the middle say its own name." These are aids that will help your children become good spellers.

## CASTING THE SPELL

Another way to help your child's spelling ability is to point out how words are made. Talk about endings and prefixes. Tell him to observe the way words look. When a child says, "How do you spell. . . ?" reply, "Try it. Think of how it looks when you read it." Give the child time to "sound out" each letter. Praise her successes and gently help her out when she gets stuck.

## SPELLING LESSONS

Have younger children call out spelling lessons to older children. You might have to whisper the word in the younger child's ear in order for him to call it out, but it makes the younger child observe the spelling and hear it as he "teaches" it to the older child. This gives the younger one a great sense of achievement, as well as helping him learn the way words are put together.

## WORD CLUES

When your child is trying to learn to spell a particularly long word, look for smaller words within it, or give a related clue to help him remember. For instance, to remember *principal* and *principle,* your *principal* is your *pal.* To remember *dessert* and *desert,* think that you don't want more than one *S*nake in a *desert,* and *S*trawberry *S*hortcake may be your favorite *dessert.*

## SPELLING CONTESTS

As your children progress in school have family spelling bees and give prizes for the winners. Have contests to see how many words each child can make from a longer word such as "Thanksgiving."

## TRY IT

When your child is reading and asks, "What is this word?" respond with, "You know. See if you can sound it out." This not only helps develop phonetics but also forces her to observe the spelling of new words. If she sounds it out and still does not know what it means, help her look it up in the dictionary to learn its meaning. Develop the dictionary habit early.

## KEY WORDS

Give your child a list of names to look up in the phone book, after he has become proficient with the alphabet. Explain key words at the top of the page. Help him practice, and praise his accomplishments as he gains this very important skill. Then show him that the dictionary and encyclopedia are arranged in the same way. Tell him he can now begin to use them all by himself. Talk about why things are arranged alphabetically.

### HONEST CHEATING

When a child is learning to spell new words for a spelling test, tell him to stare at the word for a while and concentrate on it, then to look at a blank wall and see if he can "see" the word. Then, whenever he needs to spell the word, he can close his eyes and "see" it, like magic. Tell him it's a "cheat sheet" in his head that is OK to use on a test!

## FAMILY GAMES BUILD READING SKILLS

As your children grow in their reading skills, you can further their abilities by playing numerous family games. Some familiar board games you can purchase are Scrabble, Lotto, Perquackey, Yahtzee, Anagrams, Hangman, Ghosts, and Spellbound. Many games require only the investment of time and thinking to yield hours of fun learning together.

Read poetry aloud and make up poems. Use a thesaurus to find other words with the same meaning. Work crossword puzzles as a family, looking up words you do not know. Find hidden word scrambles to do together. Make mind-stretching games a regular part of your family life.

### MAKING NEW WORDS

Call out new words you have learned and see how many synonyms or antonyms your children can name. See how many different words you can make from the same base by changing endings and prefixes.

### FUN IN A FLASH

Use alphabet flash cards for young children. Then, as the kids grow older, have them deal the cards face down. When the dealer says, "Go!" the children turn the cards face up and see who can alphabetize his hand first. The same can be done at a later stage with word flash cards.

### PARTS OF SPEECH

For a child who is struggling to learn the parts of speech, make a family game in which any member of the family can call out a sentence. The child learning the parts of speech must say who he is (the noun in the sentence). Then he must perform the action word (verb in the sentence). Even younger children who are not studying the language arts will get into this "charades" type of game and will sub-consciously learn the parts of speech.

To augment this game and learn other parts of speech, have the actor do the actions in different ways: slowly, rapidly, dejectedly, etc. These words that change or describe his action are, of course, the adverbs. Tell the child they "add to" (or describe) the verb (action).

Ask other children to call out descriptions of the actor himself: tall, short, fat, pretty, etc. These words that describe the person (noun) are adjectives. Name the parts of speech as the children learn them and repeat them often. You'll be surprised that even children in kindergarten will learn them rapidly.

## PUNCTUATION GAME

For a really fun family or classroom game, make punc-tuation costumes. These are simply a sheet of poster board cut in half, two holes punched at the top of each half, and the two boards connected by string or yarn. After the child chooses which punctuation mark he will be and prints that mark very boldly on his two halves of poster board, he pulls the cards over his neck so that he has the punctuation mark in front and in back.

Have each child dressed as a punctuation mark while the adult or teacher slowly reads a simple story with vocal em-phasis to give clues as to exclamation or question, etc. At each point in the story when a punctuation mark is needed, the child wearing the appropriate mark runs up to the story teller, turns around, and runs back to his seat. This is lots of fun in a group and teaches punctuation painlessly.

## DICTIONARY GAME

Each person takes turns being Master in this game. The Master selects any unfamiliar word from the dictionary, says the word, and spells it. Each player has a piece of paper and writes down what he guesses the definition of the new word to be. The Master writes the real definition. All the papers are scrambled and then read out loud, one at a time. Each player writes down the number of the definition he thinks is correct. Points are given for each correct answer and a new Master is selected for the next word. At the end of the game give bonus points for the person who can remember and correctly define the most new words learned during the game.

## THE FAMILY READING HABIT

Wouldn't it be wonderful if everyone kept the enthusiasm a new reader has for the printed word? Never discourage her desire to read by acting uninterested or calling the child a "Book Worm." It can be tiresome to listen to the stumbling attempts of beginning readers, but the following will help ease you and the child through this period and retain his or her eagerness to read.

By encouraging the reading habit to develop in your family, you may discover together one of the joyful pastimes of the pretelevision years. In too many homes reading is a lost art. Children must be taught by example and shown through experience that reading is rewarding and fun, relaxing and mind-enriching. Books take us to places we could never go and teach what we would otherwise never learn.

### TV LISTINGS

Teach a beginning reader to read the TV listing and to choose which programs he should watch that day, limiting the amount of time and talking to him about the content of the shows. Teach him that it is important to feed his mind as well as his body. Help him to understand that some shows enrich his brain, while other shows are not good for him.

### ORDER BLANKS

Help your youngster cut an order blank from a cereal box or magazine. Then help fill it out, printing the information and addressing the envelope. Then mail it in. This is quite an accomplishment for a young child, with built-in incentive right on the ad!

## MAGAZINES

Subscribe to magazines for your child which are his very own. Consider helping him find three other children who would like to share a subscription with him, with each family paying one-fourth the cost and keeping the magazine for one week of the month. If you cannot afford the subscription, take him each week to select a child's magazine at your library. Then make sure the child actually reads these magazines. To encourage the habit, sit down with him and read your own magazines at the same time. Read some articles from the child's magazine to him, and have him read others to you or silently. Encourage him to share the contents with other family members by telling them about what he has read.

## DAILY NEWS

Your daily newspaper is a great tool for little growing minds. Children old enough to read should begin the habit of reading the daily newspaper. Most newspapers are written on a level that fifth graders can understand and read, but the habit can be started much earlier. When you sit down with the paper, ask your youngster to sit with you and read the comics and work puzzles. Show him any interesting pictures you think he might enjoy. Ask him questions about news events and explain the basic elements of those with which he is familiar. Young children are exposed to the events of the day through television and will appreciate your explanation or discussion of them.

## NEWSPAPER GAMES

Games can be a part of the newspaper discovery, and a real boon to your child's education. Select a comic strip and cut off the words from one frame. Scramble the words and ask your children to unscramble them. Have a contest to see which child can accomplish this first. Give clues by telling the word order of the different parts of speech.

## USING HEADLINES

Have the young child cut words from headlines and paste them on plain paper to compose a letter to grandparents. Or have her compose a poem about "Me" from the words cut out.

## HALF A STORY

Tell part of a new article to a child; then ask him to find and read the rest of the article silently and tell you the rest of the story. Have each member of the family read one feature story and tell it at the family meal.

## MAKE A NEWSPAPER

Tell the six basic bits of information of any news story: who, what, when, where, why, and how. Then have the child write a news article about an event nearby. A good summer project is for the child to make a little newspaper about her friends or neighborhood. This encourages learning to type, an important skill for operating computers, too. She can type or print the stories, photocopy several sheets, and sell them door to door.

## CHILD READS ALOUD

If you have a child who is learning to read, tell him you are bored when you are all alone in the kitchen or workroom and would enjoy having a story read to you. (You can endure the new reader's oral struggle much longer if you are occupied in something you must do anyway.) If he comes to a word he doesn't know, it is easier to encourage him to "try to sound it out" if you are not looking at the page.

If he cannot sound it out for himself, ask him to spell it aloud. This forces him to notice the spelling and helps him remember the word next time. If he doesn't understand the meaning of the word, help him look it up in the dictionary or glossary of a reader, so that his vocabulary improves with his reading.

## BALKY READERS

For the child who finds reading aloud a terrible chore, sit beside him as he reads. Alternate by reading a paragraph to him and then having him read the next paragraph to you. This makes the chore much more bearable for him. Ask him to follow your paragraph with his eyes and help you if you make a mistake. Make a few mistakes to see if he is observant. Or have the child point to the words as you read them.

## PARENTS READ ALOUD

When your children are learning to read, it is very important for them to hear you read aloud. Tell them to listen as you read a sentence in a "blah" monotone. Then read it again with enthusiastic expression. The child will hear the difference. Next read a sentence one word at a time, slowly, as if it is a real chore. Then read the sentence smoothly. Tell the child she must practice letting her eyes run ahead of her mouth in order to get good expression and to read smoothly. Have her use a tape recorder weekly to record herself reading a few pages. As she listens to her own oral reading, she will try to improve each week when she records herself.

## REWARDING READERS

Encourage the reading habit. Give new readers a dollar every time they complete a book of 100 pages or more. Or allow the child to purchase a new book of his choice for every book he completes. Obviously, if you have a prolific reader already, you cannot afford to do this, nor do you need to. It is to encourage the slow reader and teach him that reading is worthwhile.

## BOOK LISTS

Keep a list of all the books your child reads. She will be proud to see it grow. These books become a great part of your child's knowledge and thoughts as she matures. It is interesting to be able to look back in later years and see how her thoughts were influenced. It is also helpful at gift time to see what subjects interest her most.

## SELECTING BOOKS

Be sure that you have appropriate books for each age. Ask your librarian and the children's teachers which are the most popular books for each of your children's ages. Check the Caldecott and Newberry Awards lists. These are awards given for the best story and the best illustrations, respectively, each year in children's literature. Your entire family will enjoy these delightful books during your read-aloud sessions.

If you have a child who declares he hates to read, perhaps he just hasn't found the right thing to interest him. Seek books about his favorite hobbies, toys, or TV personalities.

## USE PICTURES

To hook a reluctant reader try comic books, picture books, and magazines. No, these are not wasted time. Some children are simply overwhelmed with the idea of too much print. They have the feeling they will never finish a book, so why start it? These same readers may be visually oriented and while spending many pleasurable minutes poring over the pictures may read the captions almost accidentally, but they *are* reading. These kids should have the feeling that it's OK for them to lay aside magazines and short stories after only a few minutes. This encourages readers who might otherwise be afraid to tackle an entire book. Do not discourage reading in any form unless the content is detrimental. Your children may only read the inserts that come with their new toys or the ads in magazines and on cereal boxes . . . but they *are* reading.

## BEDTIME STORIES

When the child first learns to read allow him to read in bed ten minutes before turning out the light each night. An adult who does this can read about 40 books in a year!

Imagine how many books your child will read if you begin this habit when he first is excited about his new ability. If you find that stopping after ten minutes is a problem, put him to bed earlier so that he has more time to read. Instead of saying, "It's bedtime" (which demands the child's response of, "Not now!" or "Do I have to?"), you can say, "It's time to finish that good book you were reading last night. What was happening to the main character when you closed it?"

## SHARE TIME

At family meals encourage your children to talk about what they have been reading. Ask your older kids to tell one interesting item from the daily newspaper at the supper table. You are promoting conversational skills as well as training the children to read the news daily.

Have a family contest for the most books or magazines read in a month and give a prize, perhaps the purchase of a book of the winner's choice. Children take pride in owning books and are more likely to read them.

## LEARNING THE LIBRARY

Introduce your children to the joys of the library at a very early age. Make regular weekly trips there with your children. Teach them that the library is as wonderful as a free toy store, opening doors to worlds they may never visit. Help children to make appropriate selections which are not too difficult and not too easy.

## STORY TELLING

Go to story-telling sessions whenever they are in your area. If there aren't any, try to organize one for a birthday party or special treat at school. Develop the skill yourself and encourage your children to learn to tell stories with good diction, different voices for different characters, and good speech habits. Periodically, help the children to act out stories in costumes or with puppets. (For more ideas see the chapter "If I Were You.")

## RECORDS AND TAPES

Get good records of well-known storytellers. These are also available on cassettes and are found in many libraries. Listen to these sometimes during your family learning time.

## USING THE LIBRARY

Upper-elementary-age children need to learn to look up books in the library by themselves. If you have followed the tricks in this chapter, you have already established a good reading and library habit. Perhaps your librarian will take the time to show your child just how to use the card catalogue, *Readers' Guide to Periodical Literature,* and microfilm. Maybe you can arrange to have your family or some group your child is in—scouts, church, or civic organizations—take a guided learning tour of your library. If there is a college in your town its library probably has someone employed specifically to teach kids how to use a library.

Explain to the children ahead of time why the cataloguing of books is necessary and that a universal system is best to facilitate using libraries everywhere. Perhaps the children are going on vacation or to Grandmother's for a week and would like to go to the library. It's great for kids to know that the systems are similar in most libraries, so that when they learn how to use one system, they can quickly find a book in any library, with just a little help from the librarian.

Also, teach children that it is necessary to be quiet and orderly at all times in a library because others are studying there.

At the end of the tour, seat your group at a table and give each child a list of two magazine articles to find, using the *Readers' Guide to Periodical Literature,* and an old newspaper issue to locate on microfilm. Also give a subject, an author, and a title to look up in the card catalogue. Each child should have a different list. Set a time limit and then have a quiet scavenger hunt for these, with a prize of a new book or special bookmark for the one who proves to have gained the best library skills.

Finally, ask the staff to show the children what other things are available for loan. Some libraries have toys, puzzles, visual aids, cameras, videos, tape cassettes, etc. You will open a new world for those who have never known what was available. End the field trip with each child getting his own library card.

## FAMILY FUN CENTER

Create a family fun center for learning. It can be an entire room, or just a corner. Have everyone adjust their schedules so that each day the family can enjoy spending a few minutes together learning new things. Here you should have good books, including read-aloud ones, and read-alone ones for each member of the family. These may be your own or from the library. Include newspapers and magazines, too.

As your children grow, include a dictionary, an encyclopedia, an atlas, a globe, and magnifiers, records, and musical instruments. Your TV can be part of the learning center with the rule that, during the learning time, you will watch only shows that are genuine learning experiences and worth the investment of time for the entire family.

Perhaps you will be able to include other items such as a telescope, computer, microscope, camera, and tape recorder. Encourage children to bring their new knowledge from school or outings and share it with the family. But always spend a few minutes of the family learning time reading. This is an important path to knowledge and leisure entertainment which is sadly neglected in our electronic age. Too many children are growing up with the idea that reading is a bore or a chore. Show them by example and through experience that learning from the printed word is a valuable and relaxing pastime.

# IF I
# WERE
# YOU

Children of all ages adore dramatization. You probably have fond memories of the little acts you, as a child, staged for family and friends. Your children, too, will enjoy the performing and dramatics activities in this chapter and collect a lot of warm memories in the process.

While we normally think of dramas and plays as performances for an audience, there are numerous other ways the art of acting can be used to help children to learn, experience, and have fun. If you are trying to help your youngster learn a principle or change a habit, a little skit in which he deliberately acts out the correct or incorrect conduct will deeply imbed the teaching far better than any words or admonitions you could give.

The experience of acting out pretend situations can vent frustrations and feelings that would otherwise be detrimental if held inside the child or other family members. For instance, two little boys who seem bent toward starting a fight with each other, for no other reason than simple boredom or fatigue, would be delighted to have a staged fight in a little skit about the wild West. And by the end of the production, which diverts their attention and energy from their own annoyances, they will probably be best friends again.

You will find many ideas in this chapter that will help you develop your child's enthusiasm and abilities in dramatization and will teach him many concepts necessary for his safety and well-being in the process. Many other ideas are just for fun and self-expression through body movements.

## DRAMAS FOR SAFETY AND LEARNING

Dramas are an especially good way to teach safety or the handling of difficult situations to preschoolers. Tell the child first that you are going to be a bad person in the little play and that he should remember you are "play-acting." Tell him the play is to help him learn how to protect himself if he is ever in a scary situation. By creating a scene in which you represent a threat the child might encounter, he can act out different responses which come to his mind. You can discuss with him which responses are appropriate and would be beneficial to him and which ones are not correct or wise behavior. Replay the proper responses several times so that the child "practices" for emergencies or threats which could occur. This gives the child confidence and reduces anxiety levels for both parent and child.

You can also use little dramas to prepare children for difficult experiences which are a necessary part of life. You might use role-playing as a tool for teaching your teenager to put herself in another's position (maybe *yours*) before responding to a given situation. This opens the door for good communication and in many cases prevents estrangement over controversial subjects.

### GOING TO THE DENTIST

Your child might be facing his first trip to the dentist. Daddy can pretend to be the dentist and act out things the child should know to expect. This will reduce the anxiety level for the child in a new situation.

When the youngster returns from the dental office, Dad can repeat the drama with roles reversed. The child now becomes the dentist and Dad the patient. By acting the part of the dentist, the child is reinforcing things he learned about dental hygiene. He is also learning to recall and describe events in sequential order. Dad can make appropriate responses to the child-dentist, in order to open the door for discussion of his child's feelings about going to the dentist and about tooth care.

## WHAT WOULD YOU DO IF . . .?

Act out frightening situations with your child such as his first day at school, getting lost, getting sick at school, being with a babysitter while parents are hospitalized or away for an extended period of time, being seriously injured when he is alone, or being kidnapped. Repeat these dramas in the safety of the child's home and teach him how to handle various situations successfully. Ask him to improvise and tell you what he would do. Correct him if he handles the situation incorrectly. Praise his decisions if they are wise. These dramas could save your child's life someday.

## MEETING STRANGERS

To teach your child not to talk to strangers you can create many different dramatic situations. Emphasize that someone is a stranger if the child doesn't recognize the person and know his name as soon as she sees him. Improvise a situation in a store, in the yard, walking home from school or from a friend's house. Dramatize someone asking the child for directions, a stranger coming to the door when parents are not home or when parents are home. Teach the child what to do in every situation you can imagine. Repeat the dramas until the child fully understands and the correct safety actions become second nature.

## USING THE PHONE

For very young children, act out telephone conversations to teach a child how to answer a phone correctly and how to dial numbers. The child should use the real phone to practice. You can tape the button down so that the dialing does not go through and you can still receive calls. The adult should use the extension phone or a toy phone in the same room with the child in order to give help with dialing and also because it enables the child to see how the person on the other end of a telephone call conducts himself.

Pretend to be Grandmother, another parent at the office, a teacher, or a friend. Let the child practice over and over until he has mastered this necessary skill with you. Then write down the telephone number of someone the child loves and help him match the numbers with those on the phone. Practice with him until he successfully dials the numbers himself. Congratulate him. This is quite an accomplishment!

## MAKING CONVERSATION

School-age children usually need practice in the art of making conversation, especially with an unseen person on the other end of the phone. Get on the extension phone in another room. Encourage the child to ask questions and to speak enthusiastically and in sentences, instead of just answering, "Yes" and "No." Most children will even nod their heads at first.

## POST EMERGENCY NUMBERS

Help your child print emergency numbers and numbers of neighbors who are usually home to call. Together make a picture key with real photographs of the people and with pictures from catalogues and magazines to show the non-reader which number is for whom or what. Post these by the telephone to have handy at all times. The child will enjoy painting, embroidering, decoupaging, or needlepointing these numbers to frame and hang by the phone.

## TELEPHONE IN EMERGENCIES

At a young age the child should know how to use the phone for emergencies. Dramatize a situation in which the adult in charge has an accident or becomes ill and needs emergency care when only the child is present to get help. Talk about ways the child could handle the situation.

With the phone unplugged or the button taped down, have the child practice dialing the numbers and giving proper emergency information to each number until she has mastered it. She should always say first, "This is an emergency. The address is . . ."

Teach her also how to make a collect long-distance call. This is vital knowledge for a child in a case of kidnapping.

## SWITCH ROLES

Does your child have a habit you would like to change? Perhaps he complains every time you ask him to do a job, or leaves clothes and toys everywhere. In a little family drama, switch roles to show your child how he behaves. You be the child, and let him play your role. He will laugh to see his bad habits mimicked by an adult, and it will make a vivid impression on him.

Then ask him to dramatize something he dislikes about *your* behavior so that you can also improve. Tell him you will try to improve if he will. Promise to remind each other politely when you repeat the unbecoming behavior.

## GOOD MANNERS

Do you want to improve your child's manners? Do it with a little skit. You sit in your child's place at the table and have him sit in your place. You eat the meal with the same manners he usually demonstrates, exaggerating them greatly. Have him correct anything wrong he observes.

You might prop your foot on the table, sit with knees at your chest, slurp your soup, spill your drink, slam your fork down, be a picky eater, complain that you don't like the food, chew with your mouth open, talk with a full mouth, wipe your hands on your clothes, leave your napkin on the table, reach across your child for food and bump him with your elbow, etc. Talk about good manners as being simple consideration for other people.

## COMPANY'S COMING

A home drama that teaches good manners is having a "pretend" company meal *without* guests. Let the kids decorate the table with your best china, candles, and flowers. Everyone dresses up for the meal and uses his or her best manners. After a few trial runs, have a real performance with invited guests. It might be adult friends, or it could be your children's friends who are given special instructions to wear their best clothes and practice good manners.

## PLAY RESTAURANT

You also might "play restaurant" with your children at home. Dad can be the waiter and seat everyone, placing napkins in each lap. Mom can pose as waitress and take food orders.

Write out a simple menu of several choices you have available and let the children practice ordering. This is particularly good practice for teens before a first restaurant date. Include prices on your menu and advise the youngsters to practice good manners by ordering middle-priced items (too cheap indicates you believe the host cannot afford the restaurant; too expensive indicates you are a "user"). Explain the meaning of "entrée," "dinner includes . . .", "appetizers," etc.

Serve the meal in several courses so that the kids can practice using the various eating utensils with confidence. Tell what to do in the case of spills, dropping a fork, choking, or getting a piece of gristle in your mouth, and other embarrassing situations that can occur in a restaurant. Talk about using special formal manners in certain situations. Discuss what these are (boys removing hats and holding chairs for girls, standing if an older person enters, waiting until the host begins to eat, etc.)

Dad-waiter should present the bill to each child in turn and explain about figuring a proper tip, how to pay the waiter at the table for the meal in formal restaurants, and how the change is returned. Have the youngsters practice signing a pretend credit slip and including gratuities in their total "payment." Boys and girls should both learn how to do this.

Finally, practice at a real restaurant, if the budget permits. If not, help your teens to give a dressy dinner party for their friends and dates. Mom and Dad can be waitress and butler, just for fun. Each couple can bring or pay for one of the items on the menu, to keep costs low for everyone.

## PLAY LIKE

Perhaps something your child does is cruel to someone else or hurts another's feelings. Ask the youngster to "play like" that person (or animal) for a few minutes and try to feel as he (or it) feels. Then you be your child in the drama and do the unkind action you want to correct. The child will learn quickly from a few dramas like this to empathize with others and try to put himself in their shoes before he acts.

## DRAMAS FOR FUN AND ENTERTAINMENT

Dramas should not always be for teaching. They should also be a great part of your child's fun and free play. The acting he does as a child at home will stimulate his creativity, imagination, and fantasies, increasing his abilities in school, his enjoyment of life, and his appreciation of the arts.

### ACT IT OUT

Read your children a story and ask them to act it out as you read. Assign one child to be each character.

Remind your children of a favorite story they have heard repeatedly. Ask them to put on the play of that story for their dolls, their friends, or a family fun night. If you are expecting company the children might prepare the play for the visitors. The time the children spend preparing and rehearsing the play will give you the necessary time to get ready for your guests. Just confine the kids' mess to one room. And if the guests are not family, limit the performance time to prevent "audience abuse."

### HISTORY AND HOLIDAYS

To understand the reason for observing any of the various holidays, read the historical event to the children in a simplified version from the library. Ask them to plan and present a play for family entertainment on the special holiday. The drama can be a major production, taking weeks of excitement to prepare costumes and rehearse, or it can be an impromptu event with no rehearsal at all. You can simply tell the historical story during dinner and ask the children to act it out after dessert.

## FOR SMALL FRY

Have older children act out nursery rhymes for and with younger children. Have little ones chant the rhymes as prompts for the actors.

## PROFESSIONAL, PLEASE

Take your children to see a real play or professional puppet show. Going to a public theatrical production is a very special event, whether it be professional or amateur. Let the kids help select the production and go with you to purchase the tickets. Be sure it is a production suitable for children. It is awesome to children to see live actors on stage, especially if you can sit near the front. Kids will also get wonderful ideas for their own productions. Don't forget to go backstage for autographs. Children think even local theater or school actors are celebrities!

## A PARENT PERFORMANCE

You may feel no acting inclinations, but you can read a story to your children, using a different voice and a different hat for each character in the story. It makes reading time fun and shows little ones the beginnings of acting out a play.

## IMPROVISATION

Teach your children by improvisation not to be afraid to perform. Begin by giving the child a situation that he must turn into a drama. This teaches so much creativity and builds self-confidence. Perhaps the situation might be: "You are on a camping trip far from anyone else. It is just getting dark and you think you see a bear in the woods coming your way. What happens next?" Or, "You are at Disney World and there is a contest to see who is the best dancer. You really want the prize of $100, but you don't really know how to dance." Give the kids some time to create a short drama on the assigned theme.

## WINTRY DAY FUN

Give your children a box of your old (clean) clothes on a wintry day and turn on a record. Ask the youngsters to interpret the music in costumes or to act out the story they hear. Some stories are in songs on the radio, and your kids will have a great time portraying their interpretation of these. If you have a full-length mirror encourage acting in front of it. The fun could last all day.

# CREATING COSTUMES

Keep a few clothes that you would ordinarily discard. With a little alteration they make wonderful costumes. *You* probably won't even have to offer the help; the children's imaginations will take over. Look in garage sales for special costume possibilities: a ballerina tutu, a knight's helmet, an old Halloween costume of an animal or cartoon favorite. Ask a friend with older children to save outgrown costumes for you.

## NOT WHAT IT SEEMS

Some super fun costumes to improvise are:

• Mommy's nightgown can become an angel costume, a queen's dress, a bridal gown, or a Far Eastern dress with a piece of cloth or a towel for a head covering.

• A foil-covered football helmet is a knight's helmet. To make the knight's armor, glue foil on pieces cut from cardboard or from a plastic milk jug. When the glue is dry, use a large needle to sew these pieces together or onto an old pair of pajamas. Dental floss works well instead of thread. The costume will last for years.

• Do you have an old red coat? With a belt it makes a great British soldier's costume or a band outfit. A British soldier's hat can be made quite simply from an old muff, or by stitching a scrap of fake fur into a cylinder shape. Add a piece of elastic for a chin strap.

## MASKS

An animal mask is easy for your child to make in several different ways. You might use a paper grocery sack and let the child draw on it features of the animal he wishes to be. Staple or glue on cardboard ears.

Or, try a sectioned paper plate. The divisions look like a face. The child can paint on appropriate features and add cardboard ears with a stapler. A wonderful lion is made by gluing pieces of gold or brown yarn all around the edge of the plate.

Your child might create a mask from a cardboard box or a piece of poster paper.

## PAPIER MÂCHÉ MASKS

Older children will love making a papier mâché animal mask. You can get a good animal face by using a plain paper plate turned upside down for the base. Tape an inverted plastic butter tub in the center of the backside of the plate. This shape creates the muzzle of the animal. Cut away the portion of the paper plate behind the center of the butter tub. Staple cardboard ears in place.

Now soak paper towels in a mixture of one part white glue and one part water and wring them out. These towels should be placed over the butter tub and molded close to it. Completely cover the outside of the mask form with three or four layers of the glue-soaked paper. Smooth them as much as possible. Finally, punch a hole in each side of the mask. Later, you will want to insert elastic into these holes to keep the mask on your child's head.

Place the wet mask in a warm place to dry for several days. The top of a hot water heater or refrigerator works well. Good air circulation prevents the mask from mildewing. However, don't be alarmed if it does mildew; the little spots can be covered with paint or fabric when your child decorates his mask. A child will enjoy painting and adding features to his mask, which will be sturdy and durable.

## TAILS

If your child wants to be an animal figure, he can use a pair of knit pajamas for the body. If the knit top has a picture on it, have him turn it wrong-side-out or backward. Safety pin a long tail onto the seat—use rope, a cloth belt, yarn, ribbon, or whatever you have handy.

If you have some extra time and ambition you can help him sew a marvelous tail by making a long, skinny tube of fabric. Insert a piece of wire (perhaps a straightened coat hanger) which he has taped at both ends to cover the sharp points. He can stuff the tail with cotton or tissue paper and sew the open ends together. Pin the tail in place and curl it upward. The wire holds it in shape!

## WINGS

Beautiful wings can easily be made by cutting a butterfly shape from two pieces of fabric. Help your child machine stitch around three-and-a-half sides, leaving an opening for turning. After turning this right-side-out, she can insert a very sturdy wire long enough to outline the entire wings. Have her tape the ends of the wire together and hand stitch the fabric opening. Again she should machine stitch around the entire outline of the wings, about a half-inch inside the wire. Bend the wings into proper shape and position, and machine stitch a piece of bias or twill tape down the center between the two wings, for reinforcement. Use two large safety pins to pin the wings to the back of her costume.

## STAGING A PRODUCTION

Help your children improvise equipment to give a more professional look to their productions or to stage a special dramatic event for an audience. By performing for an audience, they will not only learn to overcome nervous feelings and to express themselves dramatically but will be rewarded by the wonder of applause. Listed below are some fun ways for children to make equipment from things around the house.

## PLAY MIKE

A microphone can be a wad of foil on the end of a fat pencil or black felt-tipped pen. Or help the child cut an old tennis ball and glue it to a paper towel roller. Spray it black or silver for a professional-looking mike that will be used over and over. When the children are old enough to take care of a real microphone, an inexpensive or second-hand one is a wonderful purchase. Or you might allow them to use one from a cassette player.

## LIGHTS

Use a floodlight from Christmas decorations, a big flashlight, or even a photographer's lamp.

## STAGE

Do you have a strong countertop or an old sturdy table that will hold the kids? Perhaps a trundle bed frame or a deck in the yard will meet their need. Or you can simply help them clear a corner in a room or garage.

## STAGE CURTAINS

Stage curtains can be a sheet on a string. The kids can fasten the string to the walls or tie it to chairs or door hinges. Or simply have them take the play outside and use the clothesline to hang the stage curtain.

## BAND

Is a band in order for the production? Your children will have fun taping their own background music. If you have no real band instruments the kids can make drums from various sizes of plastic bowls with sealed lids. Pot tops can be cymbals. A plastic jar of uncooked rice, macaroni, or popcorn will make a good maraca. One player might cover a clean comb with tissue paper and hum through his lips with the comb at his mouth for a tingly, harmonicalike effect.

## SOUND EFFECTS

Have the kids experiment to get the sound effects they need: water dripping, a horse galloping, or a phone ringing. Many sound effects can be improvised, and the kids will have fun discovering what sounds best.

## FIGHT FOR FUN

Do they want to fight in the play? Teach them how to do a fake fight so that no one gets hurt. If a hit in the stomach is in order, the one using his fist stops about six inches short of the other actor's stomach. The one receiving the hit doubles over simultaneously and pretends to be hurt.

If one actor is to receive a hit in the face, he should place his hand up to his face with palm exposed, on the side away from the audience. The other actor hits the open palm and it sounds and looks like a real hit in the face.

Do actors need to bleed? Fill a small squeezable plastic container (found in variety stores or where cosmetics are sold) with a little water colored with red food coloring or catsup. (Be careful to wear something that won't be ruined by the red substance and make sure that the floor and/or furniture is protected.) The squeeze bottle can be squeezed at the traumatic moment in the play.

> When performance time comes, have the camera ready. You will get some of your most treasured photos. If you have a video or movie camera, by all means, use it to record the entire performance to show your children often and for them to show their own children someday. If you do not have a video or movie camera, borrow or rent one periodically to record these treasured moments.

## MONEYMAKING BUSINESS

Not every play and performance is worthy of an admission fee. But sometimes the project could be planned with the intent to make some spending money. This is great in summer when the children have days and days to plan, rehearse, and make props and costumes.

When the children's efforts are worthy of a fee, help them print tickets. Use a photocopier.

The kids can set up a lemonade stand and make cookies and popcorn for concessions.

Posters for the event can be placed around the neighborhood and all parents and friends invited by door-to-door sales. The project can yield a good bit of spending money and lots of fun, as well as wonderful memories for your children.

Insist on an outside play for the event. Although it is not a dramatic play, a circus on the swing set is a great performance idea for which kids can develop the acts.

# OTHER KINDS OF PERFORMANCES

As your children grow accustomed to thinking dramatically they will discover many different types of performances which can be done for their own satisfaction or for the entertainment of others. Here are some ideas you might introduce to your child.

## MUSIC INTERPRETATION

Encourage a child to move freely to music for self-expression when he or she is all alone. Teach the child that an audience is not always necessary. One should be able to enjoy and appreciate his or her own performance in front of a mirror or simply by feeling, without seeing the body's movements. This teaches your child to be confident about what he or she is feeling. This confidence is important for any child's psychological well-being.

## ACTING OUT RECORDS

Plays do not always have to be long. A child's dramatic interpretation of a record is a good three-minute performance that does not wear out an audience of tired parents.

## PUPPETS HELP

Encourage the children to use hand puppets to act out favorite stories, changing their voices for each puppet.

## DOUBLE FUN FOR VIEWERS

Here is a skit that requires two children and really needs an audience. This is fun for any age of performer or audience, even adults.

To an old sheet sew a set of discarded shorts and shirt. (Any size will do, but I found that about a four-year-old size works well and is funny to the audience.) Cut a hole in the sheet at the place for each arm and leg and for the head of the figure. Reinforce these holes by rolling and stitching a hem all the way around each or by binding with bias tape, or the holes will tear apart before the skit is done. This requires a little time and effort, but the sheet for the skit can be used for years, and kids will want to repeat it often.

Two adults must hold the sheet for the performance, or tack it to a sturdy door facing, or hang it on the clothesline.

From behind the sheet one child (Jack) inserts his head for the figure's head and his hands for the figure's feet. Put shoes and socks on these hands.

Another child (Bob) stands behind Jack and wraps his arms around Jack and inserts them through the holes for the arms of the figure.

For the performance Bob's hands must do something to Jack's face. (To the audience the sheet figure looks like a humorously proportioned single person. The face [Jack's] of the figure can see what the hands [Bob's] are doing, but has no control over the actions. The hands must feel blindly for performing the action.) It is hilarious to watch as the hands attempt to feed the face, or put on makeup, or toss a ball in the air and try to catch it.

Play a record during the act and the feet (Jack's hands) can dance to the music. Every once in awhile both feet should come off the floor at the same time, or kick the face, or be held up by the figure's hands (Bob's). The performance is so funny that the children acting will want to swap places with others in order to see the act, too. To have the hands attempt to make the face up as a clown and place a wig on the head is hilarious.

## GIVE JOY

Do you know someone who is shut-in at home or in a nursing home? Encourage your children to bring joy by giving of themselves to these lonely people. Arrange for the kids to present their play or skit.

## TWISTED TONGUES

This is a fun way for older children and teens to entertain each other or younger siblings. Give the performer a copy of any simple fairy tale that is familiar to all. Tell him to read it with a twisted tongue, by interchanging beginning sounds of some words with each other.

It takes a bit of practice, but the kids will all love doing it and will surprise you at how proficient they become, usually memorizing the tale as they go. For example, "Three Little Pigs" becomes "Lee Pittle Thrigs," or a "Handsome Prince" becomes the "Prandsome Hince," a "Mud Puddle" becomes a "Pud Muddle." This performance "brings down the house" with hilarity every time!

## SPEECH-MAKING

Giving a speech is a type of performance which every preteen should practice. Perhaps your youngsters may want to be a pretend preacher or politician and mimic a dramatic one they have heard. Or they may want to imitate a historical figure and recite a famous speech, such as the "Gettysburg Address." The child may elect to memorize a dramatic poem and recite it. Help him select library books that will offer tips for making speeches. The ideas below will be useful in teaching your children this skill, which will serve them well in life.

### TELLING JOKES

Little children may begin speech-making by learning a few jokes to tell, while standing in front of the family as if on stage. Older children will enjoy learning to make speeches by sampling after-dinner types of speeches with lots of jokes from books on the subject. Telling jokes well is a skill your child will enjoy learning and for which he will be grateful throughout life.

### SPEECH CLUB

Making speeches involves certain skills you can help your child develop. It is fun to practice these skills with other children. You might help him form a speechmaking club. Have speech contests. Give awards for the child who is best in diction, grammar, voice projection, simple gesturing, eye contact, stage poise, good posture, and pleasant voice tone. If you encourage the child to memorize his speech and make a few note cards, his mind will be stimulated further.

## HEARING PROFESSIONALS

From your library get recordings of well-known speakers. Have your children listen and note the qualities they would like to develop. Or have them observe well-trained TV and radio commentators. The kids can listen to recordings of themselves giving speeches and then work toward improvement.

## SPEAKING EXTEMPORANEOUSLY

Children need to learn to express themselves clearly and forcefully in a polite manner. Speechmaking helps them develop these skills. Give your child a list of three subjects from which to choose and a time limit to plan a five-minute extemporaneous speech. He will learn, with lots of practice, to think through what he is going to say and to state his points clearly. He will learn to organize his thoughts. After much practice with this in your family setting, encourage him to do extemporaneous speeches for guests or at school.

## DEBATES

The next time two family members have a disagreement, intervene before anger rages and turn the argument into a debate. Give points for the child who can defend his position in the most politely forceful manner and who gives the most concise and clear statement of his ideas.

## PREPARED FORMAL SPEECHES

Have your child practice prepared and memorized speeches in front of a mirror and with a tape recorder. Stress relaxed and pleasant expression, body language, and eye contact with the audience. Tell your child that everyone who makes a speech is a little nervous at first. She should wait a few seconds to take a deep breath and collect her composure before beginning her speech. Then she should select a few friendly faces at the back of the room and simply "talk" to them.

# KITCHEN KAPERS FOR KIDS

Many of your family's waking hours are spent in the kitchen. Your children will invariably use it as a center of their activities, mainly because Mom and Dad are frequently there. Kids enjoy being near their parents, and you will enjoy their company as you work. For your children set aside a section of your kitchen where they can share their activities with and be encouraged by you as you do your work, and where their things will not be in your way.

Organize your kitchen (and other areas, too) for safety before your first child is able to sit up. As you organize, see things from a crawler's point of view, and from a toddler's eye level. Begin the unyielding practice of keeping anything potentially dangerous above *your* shoulder height. (It saves you a lot of bending!) Once your home is organized for safety, it takes only a few weeks to get used to where everything is kept, and you can be more relaxed about each stage of your baby's growth. By all means purchase safety caps for open electrical plugs, too. They are right at a crawler's eye level and so curiously attractive.

You might want to get the "Mr. Yuck" labels for harmful substances. These are stickers with a picture of a funny frowning face, sticking out its tongue. They are available from:

Pittsburgh Poison Center
1 Children's Place
3705 Fifth Ave. at DeSoto St.
Pittsburgh, PA 15213
(412) 647-5315

> Through their Institute for Education
> Communications (IEC), you can also order
> other educational information.

However, consider the fact that if baby is taught to stay away from "Mr. Yuck" items, you *must* label *every* harmful item and remember to put labels on new purchases of cleansers, etc., or a youngster might assume that if it is not labeled, it is safe. I think the best way is to teach baby at a very early age that he must not put anything in his mouth unless an adult says it is OK.

## LITTLE ONES IN THE KITCHEN

When he is awake, your baby will enjoy being in the kitchen near you and the activity going on in that area. Try placing his chair, playpen, or swing near the family center. The activity around him, especially if there are older siblings, will be enough to keep him content for a long while.

### TOYS ON ELASTIC

Tie some interesting and safe objects to pieces of half-inch elastic, which you tie onto his swing or high chair. He will repeatedly examine the objects with all five—sight, smell, hearing, taste, touch—senses. Don't think you have to purchase special toys for this. Try measuring spoons, old keys, various plastic or wooden kitchen tools which have no sharp edges, a giant lollipop. Be sure the items are thoroughly cleaned before you tie them on, and wash them frequently because baby is sure to test them with his mouth.

## SOCK DOLL

Make a simple doll from an odd sock stuffed with several old stockings. Tie it in the middle with a ribbon belt, and add big facial features painted on with permanent marker.

Of course, you will thoroughly clean these items before attaching them to baby's chair. Remember to clean anything you purchase for baby, too. Items collect dust and germs while sitting on store shelves.

## GOOD EATING HABITS

As your baby grows you can prevent eating problems by introducing healthful foods and keeping sweets and less nutritious things out of the home. No one needs cookies, candies, chips, sweetened drinks; and if a toddler does not develop these cravings, he will be far less likely to have weight problems later.

When you wean him to cow's milk, begin with skim milk. The fat in whole milk adds only calories, not any necessary nutrients. When you are giving your toddler finger food, try low-fat cheese, bell pepper strips, carrots, raw veggies of all types, and slices of fruit, instead of cookies, crackers, and snack foods. When you begin feeding him sandwiches, use whole grain breads instead of white. Offer water instead of sweetened drinks when he is thirsty. Offer fruits and juices for special treats. He will naturally prefer wholesome things if he has not tasted junk food.

## TERRIFIC BABY FOOD

Here is an idea which may prevent your baby from becoming a picky eater when as a toddler he makes the transition to table food. Ask your pediatrician when the time is right. Then, instead of feeding your baby commercial baby foods, give him anything your family eats, mashed or puréed according to his ability to handle it. Omit salt and heavy seasonings or spices while cooking food; these can be added at the table by family members. The entire family will enjoy watching the funny faces baby makes as he tries each new taste. Older children may even eat their vegetables as they

Watch for allergies. If any rashes or gastrointestinal disorders occur, playing detective will be easier if you have kept a record of the new food ingredients and added only one new item every four days.

encourage baby to enjoy them. Or if baby seems to like an item, big brother may be tempted to try it!

## USING LEFTOVERS

Whenever you have leftover food which is not enough to serve your family again, blend it for baby. These leftovers should be very fresh, not ones which have sat in the refrigerator for days. Place these puréed foods into homemade Popsicle holders, and freeze. Then label a plastic zipper bag or any airtight container and store the cubes until needed.

A teething baby will enjoy gnawing on these cubes to soothe aching gums. You will hear a sigh of relief as he gums the soothing and pleasant-tasting teether.

You can also freeze these leftovers in ice cube trays. The cubes can be placed in baby's warmer-feeding tray or over a pan of warm water to thaw for a few minutes before mealtime. Or they can be placed in his bowl to thaw overnight in the refrigerator for the next day. They are excellent for traveling, too. The savings you'll chalk up in about two years' worth of baby food will help pay for the vacation!

## TEACH SAFETY

Teach crawlers to stay away from the stove and from underfoot by repeatedly and quickly removing them to another, safer area where they are not in danger of burns, spills, or something being dropped on them. Make a big show of pretending to be burned by the oven and say, "Ow! Hot!" as if in pain, to teach your baby to stay away. Turn all pot handles away from the edge of the stove so that a toddler cannot reach up and pull the pot over on himself. Don't allow a crawler to be underfoot while you're removing items from the cabinet or refrigerator. You might drop something on her head.

## BABY'S PLACE

Prepare a bottom drawer or cabinet in a safe area of the kitchen for the crawler to claim as her play place. She may spend hours contentedly opening and closing the door or drawer. When she discovers that it contains interesting items she will delight in taking them out and putting them back in. These do not have to be toys. Instead, place in it seldom-used kitchen utensils which have no dangerous parts: cake pans, a sifter, a saltshaker containing a few grains of rice for noise (and no salt), and plastic pitchers.

On all other drawers and cabinets it is a good idea to keep baby-proof safety catches. But it may not be necessary if baby knows she has an area all her own. To teach and encourage her to use the area which is hers, put her blanket or favorite toy on the floor in front of her cabinet, or purchase a colorful throw rug that is just for baby, to teach her to stay in that area.

## SINK PLAY

As you work in the kitchen you may want to occupy your youngster in a place where you can watch her. Give her a sink of sudsy water and a raincoat or waterproof apron. Stand her on a safe stool and let her bathe her doll or play with a little toy boat in the suds.

## LEARNING KITCHEN SKILLS

As your little ones become more self-sufficient, curious, and mobile, they will want to know what you are doing in your activities, which are invariably above their eye level. Provide a very safe and sturdy stool for your youngster and strictly teach the necessary safety rules concerning when and where he may use the stool.

Even a toddler enjoys pretending to do what Mom or Dad does. Teach your child safe cooking habits and proper hygiene in the kitchen from the first time he or she "helps" you. Emphasize these each time, so that it becomes automatic to wash hands before handling food; never to have a pot handle protruding from the edge of the stove; not to lay paper or cloth near a hot burner; not to place hot objects directly on the counter; and to be careful with matches.

To prevent extra clean-up chores, teach your child to place the mixing bowl in the sink for stirring or pouring. Then the mess falls into the sink instead of on the counter or floor. He will probably need the stool to work in the sink.

Allow your child the pleasure of cleaning up his own mess. Of course, you could do it more quickly and thoroughly because you've had more practice. Be patient and give him the self-satisfaction and pride of doing the job well, even if it requires a few extra minutes. After all, if you take the sponge from him, you are silently saying, "I can do it better than you." The child learns to give up instead of practicing until he can do a job well.

If you allow him to leave his messes without attempting to clean up, you are teaching him to use other people and be unthoughtful. If you allow him to get away with a sloppy job, you are teaching him not to take pride in work well done. Encourage a child to do anything he can do for himself and to do it to the best of his ability.

## KITCHEN ACTIVITIES DEVELOP MUSCLES

Here are some good activities for preschoolers. These skills develop small muscles of the hands and help prepare for writing. They also promote hand-eye coordination and finger dexterity.

---

Remember, small hands need small objects to perform well in the kitchen. Cut a sponge in half; give him a small pitcher for pouring; a small, unbreakable mixing bowl, etc.

---

• **Chopping foods:** Use a chopping board and teach him to cut onto the board, not to hold the food in his hands to chop. Seat the child at a table, so there is no danger of falling off a stool. Firm bananas and butter are good for the first attempts, since the child can use a blunt knife for these. When he has mastered the motions, graduate to cheese and a sharper knife, teaching him to keep his fingers back from the cutting edge. Later graduate to celery with a small paring knife.

• **Peeling:** This is a skill which requires finger dexterity. You might begin with a carrot or celery and a peeler-scraper. Teach him always to scrape away from himself. Apples and potatoes are a bit more difficult and usually can be peeled only by elementary-age children.

After your youngsters become proficient with peeling skills, have a contest to see who can get an apple peeled, keeping the peel intact. The child then drops the peel on the counter and whatever shape it forms reveals the initial of his or her true love.

• **Grating:** Using a grater is fun for a child, but teach caution so that skin and fingernails do not get grated too. A good type of grater for a child to use is a plastic one made by Tupperware, which won't cut little fingers.

## DISHWASHING FOR FUN

Washing dishes is fun for even a three-year-old. Cover him with a plastic apron and stand him on a safe stool. You might place a nonskid bathmat on the floor near the sink to prevent having to mop up the spills. Give the child several different tools for dishwashing: a sponge, bottle brush, pot scrubber, etc., and some nonbreakable items to wash in the warm, sudsy water. He might be occupied for most of the morning with this delightful learning task.

## TOY OVEN

If your young daughter wants a toy oven and you cannot justify the expenditure, turn your electric frying pan into a perfect substitute. When she wants to cook, she can prepare batter for cakes and muffins, or mixtures for casseroles, and spoon them into waxed paper cups. She can "bake" these in the electric frying pan with the top on it (under your supervision).

## MEASURING LIQUIDS

Teach your young child to measure accurately. Mark a clear plastic measuring cup with a dark permanent marker at the one-half and one-cup marks. Have the child practice filling the cup to the one-cup mark, setting it on the counter, peering at it at eye level. Ask, "Is the water above the line or below it?" "Do we need to add more or take away some to make it right?" Use a spoon to add more water or take out some to make the measurement exact. These are excellent pre-math concepts. When he has tried the one-cup line several times, have him work on the one-half-cup mark. He will have fun pouring the water down the drain and starting over again, repeatedly.

## DRY MEASURING

Another skill to learn in the kitchen is accurate dry measuring. Of course, you should teach this with a measuring cup which is specifically for dry measurement, with the one-cup mark at the very top of the cup. Place the measuring cup in a large cake pan, to catch spills. Let the child practice measuring and leveling cornmeal, because its texture is nice and it is easy to clean up. He can scrape it level with a finger, a Popsicle stick, or a blunt knife.

Then let him practice measuring liquid and dry things with various measuring spoons. Have him experiment to find out how many teaspoons are in a tablespoon, how many fourths in a half, etc. Have him test some of the service spoons for your table to determine if they can be used as measuring spoons.

## POURING SKILLS

Another skill a youngster will adore practicing is to pour. Again, use a large cake pan to catch the spills. In it place a plastic cup to fill, and give the child a small plastic pitcher. Uncooked rice is ideal to practice pouring. When he masters this, try water, then colored liquids such as powdered drink mix, juice, or milk. For a youngster who doesn't like milk, have him pour a little into a cup and tell him he can practice pouring more when he has drunk that amount.

## ENTICING PICKY EATERS

At some stage of your youngster's growth, you will encounter his refusal to try anything new; he will eat so little it may worry you. Remember that youngsters are sometimes wiser than their parents when it comes to eating. If a child is not in a growth period, his appetite becomes markedly reduced. To force-feed or entice him with sweets will only add fat and develop eating habits that will haunt him the rest of his life.

When my son was two, he went through nearly a year in which the only foods he would eat were bananas, peanut butter, milk, and whole grain bread. He simply would not try anything else. I became very concerned and called the pediatrician after a few weeks of this. The doctor pointed out that this is a very nutritious diet and that my child could remain healthy on it indefinitely. He advised me to give a multiple vitamin supplement each day and plenty of water and to stop worrying.

If you provide your child with nutritious and well-rounded choices of food, including all the groups of food necessary for a healthy diet, and if you do not allow him to fill up on sweets first, over a period of days and weeks he will choose exactly the right foods necessary for his optimum health. Our bodies know what we need, and only toddlers seem untainted enough to listen to their bodies. We should learn from our youngsters!

However, you would not be a normal, conscientious parent if you did not want your child to try new things and learn to like many healthful foods. Here are some tricks to use to entice picky eaters, without bribing them with the promise of sweets if they eat their vegetables first.

### LEARNING NUTRITION

Even a very young child will enjoy finding pictures in magazines and helping you make a Food Groups Chart. Trace around a pie pan to make a large circle on poster paper. Divide it into fourths and print the names of the four groups: meats and eggs, breads and cereals, fruits and vegetables, dairy products. Let the child paste the pictures he finds into appropriate categories. Tell him he should have two generous portions from both the meat and the dairy groups every day, and four or more servings from the fruit and vegetable group and from the bread and cereal group every day, and drink at least six glasses of water. After each meal, ask the child to check the chart to see if he ate properly.

An easy way for a child to learn how to determine if he is eating for a balanced source of vitamins and minerals is to teach that for proper nutrition we should have different colors of fruits and vegetables each day. As you give him vitamin tablets, tell him vitamins are packaged in different colors in nature. Yellow and orange packages (fruits and vegetables) have high vitamin C. Green packages have a lot of vitamin A. Grains are a rich source of vitamin B, etc.

## HEALTHY DOLLS

Have your child prepare nutritious meals for her dolls by taking a paper plate and gluing on pictures of the correct foods cut out of magazines.

## LEARNING ABOUT TASTE

Teach your youngster about his own taste buds by a fun experiment to discriminate sweet, salty, sour, and bitter. Without letting him see the container, shake a little salt into one of his hands, sugar into the other. Ask him to lick each and tell which is salty and which is sweet. Young children have difficulty in remembering which is which. Help by asking, "Which is the taste you remember from popcorn?" "Which reminds you of candy?"

Give the child a slice of lemon to taste and experience the pinch of sour. Talk about the tingly feeling in the jaw area associated with sour. Then have him dip the lemon slice into salt and taste it again to see how the taste has changed. Next dip a slice of lemon into sugar to see the difference. Several hours later mention the sour lemon slice and ask him to think about how it tasted. Then ask if he has that tingle in his jaw.

For bitter, have the child taste a lemon peel.

Learning to taste new things helps to cure a picky eater. Have the child sample new foods and tell if they are sweet, salty, sour, or bitter. Help him verbalize which he prefers and ask him to compare the tastes of different foods.

## HIS NOSE KNOWS

To prove the importance of smell to our sense of taste, this is fun for children to do: Blindfold the child and ask if he can identify certain foods. Hold each familiar food separately to his nose and ask him what it is. Give hints until he recognizes it. Try a banana, peanut butter, grape juice, an apple, and a pear.

When he has identified correctly each food, tell him to pinch his nose with one hand and taste unidentified foods while his nose is pinched. He probably cannot distinguish between a pear and an apple. Others he may not be able to distinguish between are mashed potatoes and a mashed banana. Tell him that if he thinks he does not like a new food, he should try it first holding his nose, so that the taste is greatly diminished. Then, give it another try normally. This is a good way to help picky eaters try something new.

## LEARNING ABOUT TEXTURES

Have the child look at an array of several of his favorite foods which have markedly different textures. Several you might use are a banana, peanuts, popcorn, an apple, an orange, a favorite meat, a favorite cooked vegetable. While only looking at the foods, talk about how each food feels in his mouth. Now blindfold the child and ask him to pinch his nose closed and hold his breath as he tries to identify each food by its feeling, or texture, in his mouth.

As you offer various foods ask, "What are you eating?" Talk with him about the textures of foods. Ask which texture he prefers to feel in his mouth. Then name some food he does not like that has the same texture and ask if he will try it. Tell the child that sometimes we may like the taste of foods but not the texture. Have your child taste a raw carrot stick, and then a cooked carrot.

You will learn a lot about your child's preferences that will help you steer his appetite toward more nutritious eating. And your child will probably be more willing to try new things after the experiment.

## TRYING NEW THINGS

Have the picky eater who doesn't like casseroles to name some of his favorite foods. Try to get him to name foods that can become a casserole, such as macaroni, ham, cheese, milk, butter, celery, green peppers, etc. Then have him help you prepare a casserole using these favorite foods he has named.

Perhaps its mixed-up appearance makes him suspicious of the casserole. Eye appeal is very important to children. If, after he helps prepare this casserole of his favorite foods, he still refuses it, wait until he is a little older and try again. In the meantime, save portions of the various ingredients while making a casserole and serve these separately on his plate. Then try to get him to taste the casserole, also.

## PLAY RESTAURANT

Picky eaters who hate vegetables? Try a salad bar at home. You can chop the vegetables and store them in attractive airtight containers to be arranged around a bowl of lettuce. Include all the fancy things you find in a salad bar in a restaurant. Tell the children you are playing restaurant. The child will probably delight in the salad he makes. If not, tell him to find three things that he will eat from the array.

## VEGGIE DIP

A trick to get picky eaters to eat vegetables is to slice raw ones and arrange them around a dip. You can pour salad dressing into a bowl to use as the dip, or prepare your favorite chip dip or cocktail hors d'oeuvre dip. Children will think it is a game to select a vegetable and dip it in, using fingers to eat it and discovering that a taste with a fresh crunch is totally different than the taste of the same vegetable when cooked.

## SWEET ENTICEMENT

Offer your children some shelled sunflower seeds, co-conut, raisins, or diced dates to sprinkle on top of a vegetable salad . . . a delightful new taste which is healthfully sweet. Children think adding the sprinkling is fun and it changes both appearance and taste. Encourage them to be artistic in the arrangement of their sprinkled toppings and let them select from several choices of salad dressings, making the whole idea of salads more fun and appealing.

## VEGETABLE FLOWERS

Eye appeal is so important for enticing picky appetites. Purchase a set of utensils and an instruction book for making vegetable decorations. Encourage your child to learn this skillful art. Let her serve carrot curls, radish rosettes, turnip lilies, and squash chrysanthemums, which she has cut from the various vegetables with her very own utensils. This might become a little business for enterprising youngsters who learn the art well. Hostesses are always looking for unusual table centerpieces and hors d'oeuvres trays.

## SETTING PRETTY TABLES

Your preschooler will take pride in learning to set the table properly. There are several good ways to teach him that also promote other skills, such as learning left and right, matching sizes and shapes, observing and copying, being neat, and taking pride in what he does. As the youngster grows up, setting a pretty table becomes a special event that is associated with a family occasion. This might be for company, a special family celebration, a holiday, or just for practicing good manners.

### SET IT CORRECTLY

You might set one place correctly and ask the child to copy it at the other places. This teaches observation, right and left, and decision making.

### TRACE PLACE SETTING

Another way to teach table settings is to use white paper place mats. Set one with the plate, napkin, knife, fork, spoon, and cup. Then have the child trace around the outlines of these objects. Have him remove the mat and use it as a guide to set other places according to the pattern he has drawn. This teaches other skills such as tracing, matching shapes, and following a picture pattern.

## PUZZLE PLACE

You can help the child make a place setting puzzle that is similar to Colorforms. Cut a place mat from a bright color of flannel-backed oilcloth. Use other colors of non–flannel-backed oilcloth or vinyl to cut out the many different objects used in table settings. The child can keep these in a flat box and play with them, creating his own placements of the pieces and asking if they produce correct table settings. Give him magazine pictures of pretty table service to follow as a guide.

## USE CATALOGUES

Cut out pictures of table items from magazines or catalogues. Have the child make a proper table setting and glue it onto cardboard.

## MARK THE MAT

Purchase an inexpensive vinyl place mat in a solid color. With permanent marker or acrylic paints your child can print his name on the mat and then trace around a proper table setting. This will be his mat to use at each meal and he will set it himself.

## SPECIAL TABLES

A school-age youngster will take great pride in setting the table with all your best accessories. Let him use a pretty tablecloth or place mats, cloth napkins, napkin rings, place cards, candles, and a bouquet of fresh or artificial flowers. Offer whatever help is needed, but encourage your child to do as much as possible by himself. If you have two eating areas, the child might enjoy preparing the table on one day and then preparing a meal to serve on it the next day.

## AD IDEAS

For older children and teens, studying table settings in catalogues and magazines will stimulate their desire to create beautiful table innovations. The ideas are inspiring. Pictures also enable them to see elaborate table settings which may never be used in your own home.

## VISIT STORES

Take older children to department stores to see lovely table settings featured in bridal and china departments. They will be inspired to copy the ideas.

## NAPKIN FOLDING

Look in your library for books that show how to fold napkins elaborately. Many ideas from origami can be used. Your children will adore folding napkins to look like swans, roses, and other ideas they will discover.

## RECIPES YOUNGSTERS CAN PREPARE

As your youngsters grow they will want to try their hand at preparing recipes. With your help, they can gain skills in learning to read and follow the directions, and then they will be able to try them alone. Here are some entertaining ways to begin encouraging them in the kitchen. By the time they are upper-elementary age, they can be a real help to you. And if you lay the groundwork as fun, they will never even consider kitchen chores to be work.

## CHILD'S RECIPE BOX

Preschoolers want to cook and this is a great way to encourage them to read. Prepare a recipe card box for your child by making picture recipes. A good first recipe for a three- or four-year-old is a gelatin dessert. Draw a picture of the box mix with the brand name printed on it. Write "Pour" and show a bowl. With simple pictures and a few key words, make simplified directions for the child to follow by himself. Be sure to include all the steps in order. Add a recipe each week and let your child try it with your help. Reading and following directions is a very important skill to learn.

## SPECIAL BISCUITS

Making sausage biscuits develops a youngster's hand muscles and his self-esteem! Use one pound of uncooked bulk sausage at room temperature and about three cups of dry biscuit mix. The child can squeeze this mixture together like clay, until it is well mixed, then roll into walnut-sized balls and bake 20 minutes at 350°F. Caution him not to taste the sausage mixture until after it is cooked. If the child objects to the sausage, substitute grated cheddar cheese and sprinkle the cheese balls with a little paprika or chili powder.

## GELATIN FUN

Your preschooler will have lots of fun and feel very successful with this recipe for "gelly critters." Have him mix a six-ounce box of gelatin dessert mix with one cup of boiling water until dissolved. In another bowl, sprinkle three envelopes of unflavored gelatin over two cups of cold water and stir. Combine the two mixtures and pour into a large metal sheet cake pan, so the gelatin mixture is no more than about one-fourth- to one-half-inch deep. Refrigerate until set, about 45 minutes. Give the child several cookie cutters in animal shapes and let him cut out his "gelly critters." Lift them with a metal spatula or pancake turner onto a plate for playing. They will be stiff enough for handling for over an hour.

Kindergarten children who are learning to make letters will enjoy using a blunt knife to cut block letters from the gelatin mixture. They can "write" their names on a countertop or plate and then gobble up the letters.

Make several different colors of gelatin at the same time and let the child cut some into cubes to be used as building blocks at the table. The play is fun, and the eating yummy!

For holidays, make appropriate "gelly shapes." The child can proudly serve them with lettuce for a salad, or on ice cream, pudding, or custard for a pretty and nutritious dessert.

## HEALTH KABOBS

Ask your preschooler to plan his lunch, selecting foods from each group. Make a healthy kabob on a skewer: try slices of weiner, cheese, celery, apple, crunchy green beans, or snow peas. Serve these with whole wheat crackers and fruit juice or milk. Picky eaters will think it is great! Let them plan their own skewers, thinking of other combinations and checking to be sure the meal is well-balanced.

## YUMMY DESSERT

A good, healthful dessert that is fun for your youngster to make is quite a successful production that he can serve to his family with pride. He can spread graham crackers with applesauce and sprinkle them with cinnamon sugar. Stack these in layers. Refrigerate the stacks for several hours. At serving time, add a squirt or dollop of whipped cream and sprinkle with red hot candies.

## CHURNING BUTTER

Has your child ever churned butter? You can do it the modern way by beating whipping cream in the electric mixer until it has stiffened to butter consistency. (Omit sugar and add a little salt and a few drops of yellow food coloring.)

Or you can allow your child the fun of an old-fashioned way. Most kids will not stir with a wooden spoon long enough to make the butter, so place a half-pint of cream and a little salt in a one-pint container with a tight-fitting lid. Use a clear container so the children can see the cream change to butter. Take turns shaking the container until the butter forms. Be sure the cream is very cold. Do not store this away in the refrigerator, yet. First, let the child spread his very own butter on some warm bread to enjoy the fruit of his labor.

This churning movement promotes *gross* motor development, or strengthening of large muscles in hands and arms. Gross motor development is a pre-writing necessity.

## PARTY ICE

For a special treat in summer, allow your child to make fancy ice cubes. Place fruit chunks such as pineapple or strawberries in each section of an ice cube tray. Cover these with water or fruit juice and freeze. These are good to suck on a hot day, or to float in a glass of tea or lemonade. Mint leaves or lemon slices also make pretty ice cubes.

## MELON TREAT

Children who have learned to handle a knife safely will love making a melon basket for serving fresh fruit. Have the child use a felt-tipped marker to draw a basket shape with a handle on the outside of a melon. Then cut on the lines, taking care not to break the basket handle. The child can scoop out the pulp with a spoon, leaving the rind to hold the fruit that will be prepared. The same method can be used to create a boat by leaving off the handle. It is fun to cut the top of the melon boat in zigzags.

From the melon to be scooped out, show the child how to make melon balls, adding other types of melons for color variation. Add strawberries and pineapple chunks. The child might want to invite his friends to share his festive, nutritious treat.

## ICE CREAM

Youngsters will enjoy making ice cream, and you do not need a machine or churn for this method. Make a child-size churn by placing your favorite recipe for ice cream in a clean, one-pound coffee can. Seal the lid. Place this in a larger plastic bowl which is as tall as the one-pound can. Fill the area around the can with ice and rock salt in alternate layers. Add a little water over the ice and let the kids turn the can around and around in the ice.

Another way, which is easier for one child alone, is to place the ice cream mixture in a one-pound coffee can, seal the lid, and place this inside a three-pound coffee can. Fill the space with ice and rock salt as above. Then seal this larger can and shake it until the ice cream is made.

## THE CHILD'S MENU

Find several very simple menus that your whole family enjoys. Write the menus and the preparation instructions on index cards. The order in which things are prepared and the time allowed are very important in the instructions. Let your eight- or 9-year-old child attempt making and serving the entire meal. Read over the instructions several times with him to be sure he understands everything. Then tell him you are available if needed. See what he can do by himself.

A good menu for the beginning cook to try is:

### Tuna Casserole

1 large can tuna, drained
1 can cream of mushroom soup
1 can green peas, drained
1 32-oz. bag of potato chips, crushed

Stir together, reserving some crushed potato chips to decorate the top of the casserole. Bake in a greased casserole for 20 minutes at 350°F.

### Little Sheep Salad

For each person prepare a lettuce leaf for the sheep's meadow. Use a canned pear half for the body of each sheep, and another piece of a pear for the sheep's head.

In the small bowl of a mixer beat a three-ounce package of softened cream cheese with one tablespoon of milk. Add coconut. Spread this on the pears for the sheep's wool. Use slivered almonds for legs and horns and ears, and a raisin for each foot. Use raisin bits for the eyes and nose and a piece of a maraschino cherry for the mouth.

### Fresh Broccoli

Write instructions for preparation. To cook the broccoli suggest using a steamer, which is the easiest and most nutritious way to prepare it. The child will enjoy making a mock-hollandaise sauce for it by combining equal parts of mustard and mayonnaise and adding a little lemon juice to get the right consistency. After removing the broccoli to a bowl the child can pour the sauce over the vegetable.

### Banana Pudding

Prepare instant vanilla pudding mix according to directions. Layer vanilla wafers, then sliced bananas, then the pudding, twice. Top with a squirt of whipped cream.

---

You should have an emergency meal in mind in case the child gets tired and the project is abandoned until the next day.

---

The child should prepare the salad and dessert first, as these will require the most time and can be refrigerated while he is preparing the other two items. The tuna casserole is next and can cook while the broccoli steams. If the child tires at any point, lend a helping hand, or refrigerate the items until the next day. Remember, learning is supposed to stimulate your child's self-esteem and be fun.

## BREAKFAST IN BED

About once a month ask your kids to prepare and serve you breakfast in bed on a Saturday or Sunday. Help them plan it the day before, selecting a menu according to their abilities. Even very young children can proudly serve you orange juice and cereal. (You may have to pour some milk into a child-size pitcher the night before, for easy handling by little ones.) Even if you have to choke down cold eggs, praise your child's efforts and eat appreciatively what they bring. You are teaching thoughtfulness as well as developing the child's self-esteem and culinary skills. Be sure to do this on a day when no schedules are pressing, because you may await your breakfast for quite a long while. Beginning attempts are difficult for little hands.

## HEALTHFUL SNACKS KIDS CAN MAKE

Every child likes to make Popsicles. If you don't have the holders, invest in some. They are an investment which pays for itself many times over. In an emergency, paper cups will do, or even ice cube trays. Keep a supply of Popsicle sticks on hand, but if you run out, drinking straws can substitute. On a hot summer day, let your kids make some of these treats themselves:

- **Yogurt pops:** Combine a container of vanilla yogurt with a cup of concentrated juice. My children prefer grape.
- **Fruit pops:** Purée any canned fruit in the blender and freeze in Popsicle holders or small paper cups.
- **Bananas:** Insert a stick into half a peeled banana. Seal in plastic wrap and freeze. These are delicious plain, or can be dipped into melted Dipping Chocolate. If you have over-ripe bananas, peel them, then wrap and freeze them without a stick. Dip them in the chocolate when frozen.
- **Peanut butter treats:** Blend three cups of chocolate milk with a half cup of chunky peanut butter; freeze.
- **Special pops:** Your kids can freeze chocolate milk or pudding: Either one makes a delicious treat on a hot day. The pops can also be dipped into Dipping Chocolate.
- **Frozen drinks:** Use lemonade or any favorite colorful drink that your children like. Stand open plastic zipper sandwich bags upright in a 9 × 13–inch cake pan lined with waxed paper. Pour the drink to a height of about one-half inch in each sack and zip closed. Set the pan into the freezer. When these are frozen solid, the child can unzip the bag and use it to hold the treat as he licks it.
- **Frozen fruit:** Freeze seedless grapes or slices of bananas on a cookie sheet. When solid, package in plastic airtight containers to serve as sweet treats. These are delicious, nutritious, and very sweet when frozen. They are also

---

If you object to your children having chocolate, you may substitute carob powder in place of chocolate. Omit the dipping methods suggested.

low in calories, making them especially delightful snacks for overweight children. In summer, when grapes are cheapest, freeze a generous supply for winter snacks. It is best to pull them off stems before freezing.

• **Slush:** A special frozen drink slush your kids will love to make is a kids' strawberry "daiquiri": In the blender combine a thawed package of frozen strawberries (10 oz.), one-fourth cup of lemon juice, one-fourth cup of grenadine syrup, and one cup of cream of coconut. Blend this with one tray of ice cubes and three cups of water. Serve in parfait or wine glasses with a fresh strawberry for garnish. It makes a special party treat.

• **Salty dog:** For another favorite frozen drink slush the kids can thaw a small can of frozen lemonade, and one of frozen limeade. Place these in the blender with four cans of water and a tray of ice cubes. Serve in glasses which have a "salt-frosted" top. To do this, dip each glass rim into water and then into salt. Let them dry before pouring in the slush.

## EXPERIMENTS FOR FUN

The kitchen is the place to make all kinds of scientific discoveries. Your youngsters will make these science experiments just for fun and to watch the magic. As they experiment with these and other ideas, talk to them about scientific principles which they are observing and learning. If you do not understand these well enough to explain them, look them up together in a simplified encyclopedia or talk to a science teacher with your child. You may be encouraging another Thomas Edison in your own kitchen.

Some ideas are so old and simple that we forget, in this modern world of commercial play, how much pleasure they gave us as children. Your children will enjoy these activities and learning experiences as much as you did, and if you never tried these simple things as a child, you will have as much fun with these discoveries as your children.

### MAKE GLUE

Make real glue by mixing equal parts of flour and water. Stir to a smooth consistency. This will store in the refrigerator in an airtight container for several days.

## RUBBER EGG

Turn an uncooked, whole egg (in its shell) into "rubber" by letting it sit in a jar of vinegar for three days.

## COLORED DAISY

Turn a white daisy red by standing it in a vase of water to which you have added a strong dose of red food coloring or ink. The same can be done with a stalk of celery, if you do not have a daisy. Cut the end of the flower stem or celery stalk just before placing it in the colored liquid. It requires about three to five hours to change color.

## NATURALLY COLORED EGGS

Color eggs by boiling them in beet juice or in a pan with water and onion skins.

## INVISIBLE INK

Write an invisible message on paper by using a cotton swab dipped into lemon juice. Then iron the paper carefully to make the message magically appear. (Supervise this activity.)

---

### Buzzers Don't Argue

If your child objects to doing a necessary chore, he may argue with you about it. However, a slick trick is to tell him you are setting the stove buzzer or alarm clock to tell him when it is time to begin the task, or to tell him when he can quit. For some reason the child won't argue with the buzzer.

---

# BATH TIME: THE HIGHLIGHT OF THE DAY

I recently heard a weary young mother comment, "I hate the kids' bath time. It's the worst chore of mothering!" I couldn't believe it. The children's bath time had always been my favorite hour of the day. If you're one who hates children's bath time, you will find in this chapter ideas that will make the children adore their baths, making the chore a more pleasant one for you.

Even though your child may be old enough to bathe himself unattended, if he is sleepy or tired, you had better stay very close to be sure he doesn't fall asleep when the warm water relaxes him and makes him drowsy. I still shudder to remember finding my seven-year-old just dozing off in the bathtub. I came in to check on him just before he slid under the water. You can talk to the child from another room, asking him questions as he bathes or plays in the water. If he doesn't answer, check immediately.

Never leave a child under five unsupervised in the water.

If your child plays in the tub for a long time remember to add warm water periodically. Prevent too much heat from a bathroom heater, or a chill from a drafty area. When the child emerges from the tub he may be suddenly alarmed, as mine was when he exclaimed in horror, "Mommy, I'm turning into a wrinkledy old man!"

## LITTLE ONES IN THE TUB

I can still remember my terror the first time I bathed my first child. I was so afraid I would drop her. She seemed so tiny and fragile. I didn't want to touch her soft spot or her navel, for fear of hurting her. Every young parent has the feeling that the precious new bundle of love will break all too easily. Relax, and enjoy the fun of bathing your new baby. It can be a happy time for parents and child. Babies are not nearly as fragile as you think. In fact, they are pretty tough little beings. However, you must take care to wrap a little one in a towel or blanket as you take him from the tub, because he is very slippery and could wriggle from your wet hands very easily.

### PREVENT TEARS

An infant tub with a slanted bottom makes the task of bathing baby so much easier. Use your elbow to test the temperature of the water since your hand is already toughened to hot water. Because the infant tub is shallow it keeps baby's chest out of water.

Many babies cry during their baths. If you imagine yourself wet and sitting with your body out of water, you'll discover the reason for baby's screams. You get cold very quickly. So does baby. Be sure the tub is in a warm, nondrafty place. Use a little plastic cup with a handle—a plastic measuring cup works nicely—and pour the water over baby's chest and stomach frequently. Or soak a clean, cloth diaper or baby towel with warm water and lay it over baby's chest while you bathe him. Wring the cloth with more warm water as it cools down.

## SEE THE BABY

When baby is old enough to sit up, place the tub in a warm, nondrafty place in front of a mirror. He will adore watching himself as you bathe him. In the mirror he'll also see you, making *two* of his favorite person! Let him sit watching himself for awhile before you bathe the part out of water. Then wrap him quickly to prevent a chill.

---

When changing baby's diaper, prevent diaper or heat rash by using what Great-Grandmother used on her babies—cornstarch instead of powder. It is softer and works better.

---

## NAIL CARE

The best place to cut children's fingernails and toenails is in the bathtub. The nails are softened from the water and much easier to trim. The child is usually occupied with water play and won't resist you so much. Purchase a soft nail-scrubbing brush and show your child how to use it. Keep it handy when he is bathing. It will be fun for him to dig his fingernails into a bar of soap, leaving a funny impression, and then tickle his hands with the brush to remove the soap particles from his nails.

## TEACHING TIME

While you are in the bathroom allowing your youngster to enjoy the water, if you are pressed for time you can make grocery lists, write letters, or read a magazine or the next chapter of this book. Use rubbing alcohol on a paper towel to make your bathroom fixtures hygienic and sparkling in a jiffy as you talk to your little one. Remember, this is an opportune time to talk to your child, read aloud to him, say nursery rhymes, and give him good messages about himself to promote self-esteem.

## COUNTING GAMES

During baths, play counting games with little fingers and toes. Repetition makes learning to count easy.

## BODY CONCEPTS

Bathtime is the perfect time to teach a toddler the names of the parts of the body. It is important that your child's early concepts of body- and self-image are positive. You can teach modesty without making him ashamed. You should teach the child as soon as he or she is old enough to understand that the area beneath his or her underwear is personal and belongs only to the child. Teach a child who is old enough to be toilet trained that he or she has the right to say "No" if anyone tries to see or touch the personal area, and that it is vital for him or her to tell you if anyone ever does try this. But do not transmit fear. Remember, you are teaching a child concepts about self that will affect all relationships with people and will set the tone for sexual relationships in adulthood.

I have co-authored a book to read with your children, *Do You Have a Secret?* (by Pamela Russell and Beth Stone [my pseudonym], CompCare Publications, 1986). This picture book opens the door for talking about difficult subjects with your child in nonthreatening ways. You can get a copy from your local bookstore or by calling toll-free: 1-800-328-3330. Another good book to read with your youngster is *Private Zone,* by Frances S. Dayee.

## PREVENT ACCIDENTS

Watch your toddler at all times in the tub, but do not teach him to be fearful of water by constantly saying, "Be

---

Of course, you will teach your young child never to touch electrical switches, plugs, or appliances while in the tub or while wet. Keep these out of reach, lest he forget. Teens need also to be reminded of this periodically. It is a wise idea to use even hair dryers in the next room.

careful." Instead, teach him that standing in the tub is not allowed. Have your youngster help apply decorative decals to the bottom of the tub to prevent skids. (These are available in many stores.) Tell your child these decorations are little signs that say silently, "Don't stand up!"

## SHAMPOO TRICKS

For shampooing very young children, it is often easier to use a kitchen sink equipped with a sprayer. Use a rubber dish draining mat, and pull it several inches over the edge of the sink. This directs the water back into the sink. Lay a thick towel over the part of the mat that is on the counter beneath the child's shoulders, and let the hair flow down over the draining mat, so that the child's head is still supported by the counter. You can wear a plastic apron or raincoat, to prevent having to change clothes afterward. Be sure to cover your child's body, because she can get a chill from having wet hair.

Be sure to use a shampoo that does not sting the eyes. If your little one hates shampoos, a hand shower which attaches to the tub faucet is ideal, if you can find one to fit your faucet. These are available in hardware stores and are well worth the expense. Read on to discover some tricks and diversions which can make shampoos fun instead of a battle of the wills.

### EARPLUGS

When my four-year-old had ear surgery, I discovered a wonderful device I wish I had known about earlier. Swimmers' earplugs, which can be purchased in pharmacies or swim supply shops, can prevent much of the fear of shampoos, as the water doesn't get into the child's ears and clog them. If your child objects to these at first, play a little game. Ask her to see if she can tell what you are saying with the earplugs in her ears. (Of course, if you speak in a normal tone she will be able to hear you, but you will only mouth the words for this game.) Have her watch your lips as you shampoo her hair, and mouth the words, "I love you." She will concentrate on your lips and forget that her hair is being washed.

## PLAY BEAUTY SHOP

As the child gets too big for the kitchen counter, encourage her to shampoo herself. Give the child a small, unbreakable mirror (highly-polished metal ones are available in the parakeet section of pet stores). Or better still, mount a full-length mirror on the wall opposite the tub. Tell her to play "beauty shop" while her hair is still soapy. She can pile her hair high on her head, twist it into weird shapes that stand out on her head, and with every new creation, she will be cleaning her scalp and hair.

## PITCHER FULL

When it is time to rinse, tell her to lean her head back as far as possible and see how long her hair will stream down her back. (Little girls love to pretend their hair is down to their waist in back.) This backward movement makes rinsing easier and keeps the water out of her eyes. If you have no hand shower, use a large plastic pitcher to pour the water over her head, placing the lip of the pitcher at the scalp line on her forehead, so the water runs backward. Have the child rub her scalp for you as you pour the water. If you need to divert her attention, have her count for you how many pitchers full it takes to rinse her hair completely.

## EYE PROTECTORS

A little boy who continually complains about water running into his eyes will be content to wear a stiff plastic sun visor on his forehead during the rinsing, or to hold a folded washcloth over his eyes. It's also fun to wear swim goggles.

## BATH TIME, FUN TIME

"I don't want a bath!" A tired, impossibly cross child can turn into an angel in the bathtub, once you get him in there. Don't *you* feel better when you can submerge tired muscles in a warm soak? But getting the cranky child into the tub can be a problem. Here are some wonderful ideas for bath time play that can coax your youngster into the tub and occupy him for those thirty minutes before supper, when he is too cranky to bear.

## JUST LIKE DAD

Boys enjoy lathering their faces with a little no-tears shampoo and pretending to shave while looking into the mirror. Give them a toy razor or an old razor holder with the blade removed. But be sure you do not keep your real razor within reach of the child, because he might use it by mistake.

## BUBBLE BATHS

For boys, a mild liquid detergent works great and is cheaper than commercial bubble bath. Purchase a plastic bottle of it for the tub and let the boys paint a face on it with permanent markers to designate it as theirs.

Tell your girls they are special because they get to enjoy the luxury of bath oil. They will have fun making it themselves by adding cologne, or scents used in candle making, to some baby oil, or even cooking or mineral oil. Bathe the boys after the girls because bubble bath cleans away the oil residue in the tub.

---

A bubble bath for boys is great fun, but pediatricians tell us it promotes urinary tract infections in girls.

---

## BUBBLE FUN

Your kids can enjoy another type of bubble fun in the tub. Have you ever had permanent spots in your furniture or carpet from bubble-blowing liquid? The bathtub is the best place to use it, if you can't send the children outside with it. They will also enjoy making their own bubble-blowing liquid from one-third cup of dishwashing liquid, three-fourths tea-spoon of cooking oil, and one-half cup of water.

This is also perfect rainy day fun in a dry tub, with several fully clothed children playing together. Just remove their shoes so that your tub is not scratched, and remove their socks to prevent slipping. Also remind them that standing in the tub is forbidden.

Let your children experiment with different bubble tools. Try an old spool, a strainer, drinking straws, an old smoking pipe (which you have washed thoroughly), a large washer, a plastic strawberry basket, and many other things the kids will think of. Let them make bubble-blowing wands by twisting pipe cleaners into various shapes. To blow multiple bubbles bend the pipe cleaners into adjoining circles like a three- or four-leafed clover.

> Soak tub toys in a pan of water with Mr. Bubble added to get them clean easily. Then soak them in vinegar or rubbing alcohol and remove all soap residue with a scouring brush.

### IN COLOR

Sometimes a toddler might enjoy a blue, green, or red bath. Use only a few drops of food color so that skin will not discolor.

### MELTY SOAP?

Does your child "melt" a bar of soap with each bath? A good remedy is soap on a rope to tie to the faucet. You'll find it in giftwares for men. Kids will also enjoy making their own, which works even better.

Have the child cut a thick washcloth in half. Then fold one piece in half and stitch it into a little pillowcase. At the open edge fold and stitch a one-inch hem into which she will insert a drawstring of quarter-inch-wide, soft elastic. The elastic should be cut to about ten or twelve inches in length and stitched together, so that when the bag is pulled shut, the elastic forms a handle to fit over the wrist. Insert a bar of soap into the washcloth bag, then draw the elastic tight. Now your child can fit the elastic handle over his wrist, bathe himself, and hang it on the faucet until his next bath. It's also a good way to use all those small bits of soap that are left from each bar. Just fill the bag with leftover soap bits.

## FUNNY FACES

Little girls will enjoy applying make-up in front of the tub mirror. Tempera paints on cotton swabs are fun for little boys to paint themselves as Indians, clowns, etc. They can wash their faces before emerging from the tub.

## POUR MORE

Give your child a plastic cup and a small plastic pitcher and let her practice her pouring skills in the tub, where spills don't matter. Tell her to listen to the sound as the cup fills. If she listens closely the sound will always tell her when the container is full. Have her experiment with her eyes closed. Tell her this is how blind people know when something is getting full.

## WHAT FLOATS?

It is interesting for preschoolers to discover for themselves what will or will not float. In the tub you can teach beginning principles of science. Ask your child to collect several items of various materials before bathtime. During his bath he can test each and tell you what will float. Ask the child, "Is it the shape, or the material used, or the weight of an object that allows it to float?" Experiment with a solid metal toy and then a plastic or wooden one of similar size. Be sure to remove metal items as soon as they are tested so they won't rust, or scratch your tub.

## WET PAINT!

Are you one who really encourages creativity and self-expression? Or are you really desperate for terrific entertainment and don't mind a mess to clean up? Here's a great activity your kids will talk about until they're grown! Bath wall murals! You can purchase crayons especially made for this, or you can improvise several different media with your kids.

Try old discarded lipsticks and eye crayons, tempera paint, nonpermanent felt-tipped pens, washable crayons, and food coloring on cotton swabs. For finger painting on the tub walls, try this marvelous mixture: straight liquid starch mixed with a little tempera paint. This mixture makes a type of fingerpaint that the kids will adore. They can also do body painting with it, and it will all wash off easily. You might end this play with a shower to remove most of the color, followed by a good bath in which the kids wash the walls as well as themselves. Rubbing alcohol on a paper towel will clean up the mess in a hurry.

## BOATS AND MORE BOATS!

Every child loves toy boats in the tub. They can be expensive to buy, but your children will have more fun with the ones they make. And in creating their own boats, the kids' imaginations will grow far more than if they follow the instructions on a commercial boat, which used someone else's imagination. Here are some ideas for your child to try:

### WOOD STACKS

Suggest that your youngster make some boats out of wood scraps. You can request these free from a building site, lumberyard, or cabinet shop. The child can spend hours out of the tub stacking various sizes of wood and nailing them together, or gluing them with carpenter's glue. If he decides to paint the boats, do not give him tempera paint, as it will wash off. Model paints and acrylics work well, or simply use leftover house enamels. *Permanent* markers also do nicely, if you don't want the mess of paint.

### PLASTIC BOTTLES

Your child can make another kind of boat from a large, clean, plastic bottle. (Be sure to select one which never contained a toxic substance.) Help her cut the bottle in half with some sturdy scissors. Then she can cut the boat in any shape she desires—perhaps a shallow boat with a tall sail made of the leftover plastic pieces. Older children may want to use Popsicle sticks or dowels to insert as masts, adding intricate string riggings and cloth sails.

## NUT SHELLS

For other bath toys, try walnut and hickory shells which float and make adorable little sailboats when your child adds a piece of a drinking straw or cotton swab as a mast and a little cloth sail.

## BAMBOO CANOE

Find a piece of bamboo and help your child cut it in half for a lovely canoe for his little toy people.

## STICK RAFT

Your child can fasten several sticks from the yard or Popsicle sticks together with string or glue to make a raft.

## CARVED BOATS

A child who can handle a knife safely can carve a little boat from a piece of balsa wood to float his small toy animals. Or simply use an appropriately shaped piece of plastic packing foam from a dumpster behind an electronics or computer store.

## BALLOON BOAT

Plastic butter tubs make cute boats. You can add a sail. Or try this: Help your child punch four holes at equidistant intervals around the top of the butter tub and insert four strings of equal length. He can tie these to a helium-filled balloon for a little hot air balloon and basket. The child can put a few little toy people in the plastic bowl to weigh the balloon down just enough to make it sail on the water surface when he blows on the balloon. As he takes the figures out, the balloon will rise into the air a little.

A variation on the same idea is possible even when you have no helium balloons. The child can make a parachute for the little toy people. Attach the strings to the butter tub and then to four corners of a piece of plastic cut from a bread wrapper. The parachute will not rise off the water but will land on it when your child holds it in the air and drops it.

## CREATING TUB TOYS

Your children can make lots of toys for the tub out of things you normally have around the house or things you might discard. Take a little time to help them get started, then watch their imaginations turn the most ordinary thing into the most extraordinary and special tub toy.

### CREATIVE FREE TOYS

Instead of expensive tub toys, give your child an assortment of clean, discarded plastic bottles. Let your child's creativity take over. He will probably turn the trigger type bottle into a good water gun. Empty plastic bottles with tops tightened are imaginary boats. He can use bottles with handles for pouring. The caps of different sizes and shapes make rafts for little plastic animals and people. Your child's imagination will surprise you. Unfortunately, many commercial toys discourage creativity.

### BOTTLE PUPPETS

Children like to play with empty plastic bottles in the tub. Do not give them any bottle which held a toxic substance because the residue may harm the child. A funny finger puppet for the tub can be made from a large plastic bottle, perhaps a Mr. Bubble bottle, with the label and cap removed. Turn the empty bottle upside down and place the child's middle finger inside. It becomes a huge finger puppet. Your child can add facial features with a *permanent* marker. He can also use Elmer's Glue-All or any strong white glue to add yarn hair and some ears cut from a piece of another plastic bottle. The glue should dry for a couple of hours before the puppet is used.

### CARVING

A fun creative craft in the tub is soap carving. Give your child a blunt plastic knife and a bar of soap which he softens in water. In the tub, he can carve a toy of his own. While carving is easier in the water with the softened soap, the resulting creation can be dried and kept as a masterpiece on his shelf. If you use Ivory soap, whatever he carves will float. Caution him to hold the blunt knife only while seated.

## SEE THE SEA

Perhaps your children have never seen the ocean and you would like to explain what it looks like. Or maybe their favorite vacation was a time spent at the beach and now, they wish for the sea again. They can make their own miniature ocean in a large, clear plastic bottle with a good twist cap. Fill the bottle half full with water that has been tinted a pretty blue-green color with food coloring. Then fill the bottle to slightly overflowing with cooking or mineral oil.

Secure the cap tightly, and wash the oil off the outside of the bottle. There will be many tiny bubbles trapped inside the bottle, and these create the appearance of ocean foam. Turn the bottle on its side. As you gently rock it from end to end a miniature wave will roll within your little ocean. This is an excellent tub toy. Your child can keep it on a board covered with sandpaper and a few shells as a decoration for his room.

## PUPPET MITT

A hand puppet washing mitt is great! Make it from a worn towel, or from two cheap washcloths that are not thick. A child five or older will enjoy helping to make it himself. Cut the two pieces in the shape of a fat "t" similar to a hand puppet. With right sides together, help the child zigzag stitch the two pieces together, leaving the wrist area open. Turn it right side out.

Your child can decorate the puppet mitt with facial features and clothes by sewing or gluing on knit material in desired colors. A good fabric glue (I like Sobo) suitable for washable items will hold in the bath. Use knit fabrics for the features. Like felt, these will not ravel, and they have the advantage of being colorfast and washable. Washable yarn is good for the puppet's hair.

This mitt can provide hours of happy, wet play. The undecorated back of the puppet is a washcloth that is easy for little hands to use. If you leave the mitt as a toy in the bathtub, be sure to wash and rinse it thoroughly every few days.

## SWIM PRACTICE

The bathtub is an excellent place for preschoolers to learn swimming readiness. Stay in the bathroom with your child and encourage the techniques you will discover in this section. Praise his performances. Children love an appreciative audience.

To interest the child in the principles of swimming, first, encourage him to make little floating friends for his bathtub play. Save corks of various sizes and shapes from empty bottles or purchase some from fishing supply shops or hardware stores. The child can cut these to desired shapes with scissors and glue the pieces together to make "The Bobsy Family" . . . little floating friends. Make facial features with permanent markers. Tell your little one to watch how the floating friends can stay on top of the water and swim. Say, "You can learn to do this, too."

### BELLY UP

Encourage your child to lie on his back and completely relax so that the water covers all of him except his face. Tell him to stretch his nose and his belly button upward toward the ceiling. This is the beginning of the back float. Begin with shallow water and add more until he is really floating.

### BUBBLE TALK

Ask your child to lie on his tummy and practice taking a deep breath and blowing bubbles in the water. Encourage him to put more and more of his face under the water as he blows. Teach him to exhale through his nose under the water to prevent the bubbles from tickling his nose.

If he is reluctant to blow bubbles, tell him to take a breath, put his mouth underwater, and talk to hear how funny he sounds. This accomplishes the same thing as blowing bubbles but diverts the child's attention by having him listen to himself.

## SPLASHING FUN

Gently splash water in the youngster's face and make it a fun game, not something to fear. Wear a raincoat to protect your clothing, and remember that the bathroom floor will clean up easily. Encourage him to use the sprayer on his face or hold his breath and let the shower flow in his face like gentle rain. Getting accustomed to water in his face prepares him for swimming.

## KICKERS

Have the child lie on his tummy in the tub and kick with his feet in regular up and down motions. Have him lie on his back and practice the frog kick.

## PLAY WINDMILL

Sitting in the tub, your little one can practice swimming arm motions by pulling his bent elbow back as far as possible and then stretching his hand as high as possible and bringing it forward and down again with fingers "stuck" together. Alternate arms. Tell him he is playing windmill. For a child who is afraid of swimming call this "water exercise," not "swimming." When he can do the arm movements successfully, ask him to kick at the same time, while sitting in the tub. This will be difficult to learn but fun.

## CLEAN UP TIME

You may have had trouble getting your child into the tub, but with the fun he has had there (if you used some of the ideas in this chapter), you will probably hear loud objections when it is time to get him out of the tub. The splashing and fun has probably created quite a wet floor and left some cleaning up to do. If you make a game of it, the child will learn to clean up his own mess and think it is fun. Here are some tricks to try.

## DRIPPY TOYS

For bathtub toy storage, if you cannot afford to purchase the plastic racks available, or if you have a molded plastic tub wall with a ledge on only one side, use a mesh bag from a turkey or citrus fruit or use a plastic mesh swim gear bag. Teach your child to place all wet toys in it and hang it over the faucet to drip dry. Tell him the toys are tired and need to go into their little bed to rest. He may kiss each one good night and tell it he will be back to play tomorrow.

## CLEAN UP

Make a tub flower by cutting a long strip of nylon net five inches wide. Fold it in half lengthwise and gather the double thickness by stitching the cut edges together. Pull up gathers and stitch the ruffle ball together, making a scrub puff, which looks like a little flower. The child will be delighted to have several flowers to float in the tub.

If the child is reluctant to leave the tub fun, it is easier to get her out after the water is gone. You can have her play this little game as the water goes and teach her to wash away her own bathtub ring at the same time. Tell her to pull the plug on the drain and race Miss Drain to see if she can use the tub flowers to rub away all the bathtub ring before Miss Drain drinks all the water.

## DRYING OFF

Tell your youngster to pretend to be a little dog and shake all the water off onto the mat, while drying with the towel. Laugh at his doggie antics. Ask if his feet can play monkey and move the mat around to dry the floor.

## TOWEL UP

From age three a child can learn to hang his towel and leave the bathroom tidy. He is capable of doing the task, but you must teach him to be thoughtful by practice. Pretend there is a giant dragon who eats towels that hit the floor.

For a hand towel for your preschooler who cannot reach the towel bar, use a large hanger clothespin (sold for travel) which hangs over the towel bar like a coat hanger and has a long clothespin to clip the towel in a low position for the youngster to reach. Small fry don't have to remove the towel or rehang it. Or you might use Velcro or large safety pins to make a bath towel that becomes a continuous towel roll around the towel bar.

## PRETEENS AND TEENS

As your child outgrows toys in the tub you can encourage other types of bathtub fun, learning, and creativity. Talk about maturing bodies and modesty. Respect your preadolescent's privacy in the tub. It is a good place for the youngster to read an appropriate book about growing up, personal hygiene, and beauty tips.

### GET A TAN

If you have a fair-skinned teen who wants to tan, put some orange or brown food coloring in the bath water to stain the skin a little. She can experiment with the amount.

### BEAUTY CONSCIOUS

Give your preteen a book or magazine with manicure tips and purchase the necessary items for this important grooming procedure. Young ladies will enjoy giving themselves manicures and pedicures in the tub.

### TUB-ERCISE

Does your youngster hate to do exercises because she sweats? Show her some that can be done safely in the tub or under a cool shower. Isometrics work well. Get a book to show her how to do them.

### EXERCISE

If you can afford to purchase some exercise equipment and can find a corner of a room to designate as the "gym," your entire family will benefit from fitness competition. Make charts and have contests with each other to see who does the most sit-ups in a week or runs the most miles in a month. Always follow vigorous exercise with a warm bath or shower to prevent sore muscles.

## LEARNING TIME

If your adolescent enjoys relaxing in a tub for a long, leisurely bath, suggest that it is a good time to listen to a self-help tape or to learn a foreign language just for fun. But caution again about not touching electrical appliances, radios, cassette players, or a heater switch while wet. You taught the child all this when he or she was very young, but teens sometimes seem to leave their brains at school!

## NATURALLY FRESH

With a good library book from the section on natural products, pioneers, and unusual recipes, encourage your teens to make some hygiene or beauty products in the way Grandmother made these items before they were available commercially. Old-fashioned soap and shampoo making could be the entertainment for a girl's spend-the-night party. Healthful face scrubs and beauty tricks from nature will fascinate any teen.

## LIQUID REFILLS

Kids have fun making soft soap to refill commercial dispensers. Keep old bits of bar soap in a jar of sterile water to soften them. Add a little glycerine and a few drops of cologne and whip in a blender.

## FANCY BARS

Girls will enjoy making fancy bars of soap by cutting pretty designs from greeting cards and gluing them with white glue to one side of a bar of soap. Sweetheart soap has an embossed border which they can paint with gold paint or fingernail polish. When the design is dry, shellac or coat it with plastic spray or clear nail polish. The design will last until the soap is used up. Old Valentines also have perfect pictures to use on the soap. These fancy bars make a great gift for Teacher or Grandmother.

## PERSONAL HYGIENE

By all means, show young shavers how to use a razor without injuries. Many preteens think it is necessary to scrape hard with a razor. This definitely leaves a raw shin-bone for that first pair of hose!

Teach your preteens about using deodorant and other personal hygiene products. Purchase different brands for them to try and observe if any skin irritations result from some brands. *You* have a preference for certain brands; allow your children to choose the ones best suited for their skin also. Their choices may be different from yours. Teach the youngsters not to share these items. Each youngster's favorite brands make good stocking fillers at Christmas.

## FACE CARE

Preteens who are just becoming aware of acne will listen carefully to facial care instructions. This is the best time to establish the practice of keeping the skin scrupulously clean. If you have a friend who has especially beautiful skin, comment on it when your teens are present and ask the friend what she does for facial care. The chances are the answer will be drinking lots of water and keeping the skin scrupulously clean. Your teen will take note much more readily from the friend's comments than if you constantly admonish the youngster to wash her face.

## GIVE ENCOURAGEMENT

Compliment these growing youngsters often about the good habits they are developing. It will encourage these habits to continue. Your teen has a great need to feel approval from others for his emerging new physical self. It is very important at this stage for your child to receive compliments whenever they are merited. And do not criticize your child unless you feel it's absolutely necessary. A child's self-image is very fragile at this age. A positive self-image is vital for your grown-up youngster's sense of well-being.

# LOVING
# NATURE
# IS NATURAL

How much do you know about your world and the things you see every day in nature? We usually take for granted the things with which we have grown up and do not bother to learn about them. Now is the time to learn, *with* your kids. In this chapter you will read about many ways you can study nature with your children. They will probably ask you many questions as you awaken their little minds to the wonders around them. Get a good nature guide book which will help you answer their questions. I like to use the Golden Press nature study books because they are inexpensive and small enough to keep in your car or purse. Each is on a different subject: Trees, Birds, Flowers, etc. The illustrations are good and the wording is easily understood.

## FUN WITH NATURE

There are many games of discovery that will incite your child to be aware of flowers, trees, seed pods, etc. Each time you do something innovative with a particular plant, impress the name on the child's mind and have him repeat it several times. Have him help you look it up in your nature book. If you regularly do activities such as the ones listed here, your child could be at the top of his botany class in high school, without even studying!

## NAME THE FLOWER

Help your child pinch a snapdragon blossom and watch the dragon snap open its mouth. Ask your youngster to guess a name which might be appropriate for the flower, or to notice how the flower might have gotten its name.

## LITTLE HELICOPTERS

On maple trees in the spring are little winged seed pods. Tell your child to sail these through the air like little helicopters. He is helping to spread the seeds for future trees.

## CHEWING GUM

Help your child find a sweet gum tree and cut a small place to make the sap run. This is old-fashioned chewing gum. Look in your Tree Book to be sure you have the right tree before tasting the sap!

## HIDDEN STAR

Give your youngster an apple to cut around the equator, instead of from stem to stem, and see the perfect star inside.

## BLOW IT AWAY

In summer be sure your youngster makes a wish as he blows dandelion seed to the wind. If all the fuzz is gone in three blows the wish should come true! Or count the number of blows for a dandelion to tell what time it is.

## SWEET DISCOVERY

Don't forget to suck the honey from honeysuckle and verbena by removing the green calyx at the base of the blossom and sucking the drop of nectar there. Be sure your child can properly identify honeysuckle. Some children confuse yellow jasmine with honeysuckle, and jasmine is deadly poisonous.

The best rule to teach your child is to taste things in nature only *after* checking with you, or with a plant authority.

## BABY INSIDE

Soak any dried lentil (lima, black-eyed pea, pinto, etc.) in water for a few minutes until it can be easily separated into its two halves. Inside, your child can see a perfect baby plant with two tiny leaves, which would emerge above ground if the lentil had been planted.

## PELLET GUN

Kids love to shoot the heads of foxtail weeds like a pellet gun by wrapping the stem in a loop around the head and snapping it suddenly, sending the head flying into the air.

## MAKE A PIG

With your child find the green fruit of maypops to make into little pigs, by inserting sticks for feet and attaching a smaller fruit for the head.

## SQUIRREL'S SUPPER

Have your little one pull up a new oak seedling and see the acorn which has sprouted.

## LITTLE DANCER

Little girls love to turn large, lavender passion flower blossoms upside down and remove the stamen until only two remain for the feet of a little ballerina. The flower petals look like a lovely tutu.

## FIT FOR A QUEEN

Do you remember how to make a clover necklace? Teach your child, too. If you never had the pleasure, the way to make one is to pick the flowers with stems several inches long. Near the bottom of the stem make a length-wise slit with your fingernail or a needle. Insert the stem of another flower and pull it through until the flower head rests at the slit. Continue to add to your chain until it is the right length for a queen's crown or necklace. If you live in a city, purchase an inexpensive bunch of daisies for your child to make a necklace.

## MAKE A LEI

Large, open blossoms such as day lilies, hibiscus, or althea make a lovely lei. Cut the flower heads without stems. Simply use strong thread on a large, blunt (crewel embroidery type) needle to pull through the centers of the flower heads, making the leis as long as desired.

## LUCKY DAY

Have you and your child looked for four-leafed clovers together? This is such fun and a wonderful pastime when the child has nothing to do. And, who knows? Maybe they *are* lucky. I have framed over my desk a very large four-leafed clover which I found on the day I received the contract for this book!

## LEARNING ABOUT TREES

Trees are vital to our environment, yet we often take them for granted. If you live in a city and trees are not plentiful, you probably appreciate them more than those who live in rural areas. You might take your children to a park, nursery, or greenhouse. Help your children learn to respect the value of trees and to discover them as friends. Even a city child can learn a lot about trees and have fun with the activities in this section.

Tell your child that trees are alive. There are even some people who believe trees communicate with each other and that they like people to rub them and talk to them. Every living thing thrives on care and attention.

## TREE WALKS

What kind of trees and shrubs are nearest you? Purchase an inexpensive, pocket-size book about trees and a small, unlined spiral notebook. Gather all the kids and go for a "tree walk." Collect as many different kinds of leaves as you can find. Have the children really look at each different kind of tree, walk around it, stand back and look at its full shape and size. Observe the different shades of color in the leaves.

Talk about the way a tree is propagated. If you are walking in the spring, you will be able to collect the flowers or seed pods, which may be winged little airplanes. In fall you may find nuts, berries, or cones. Ask the child to figure out how these seed pods are spread from one area to another. Some are carried by wind on little wings; some are eaten by birds and go through their digestive systems to be redeposited in another area; some are hitchhikers and take a ride in the fur of an animal; some are planted by squirrels. Talk about these ways of nature. Your children will be fascinated with the plan. Their imaginations will be stimulated as they later observe newly sprouted trees which are far away from parent trees.

## MY TREE FRIENDS

When you walk in the fall, collect various colored leaves and evergreen needles to take back home. Have the children make a scrapbook titled "My Tree Friends." Your child can encase each leaf in two pieces of wax paper and press with a warm iron. (Protect your ironing board with a towel.) Then help her look up the leaf in your tree book and write its name as she mounts the leaf on its page of the scrapbook. Perhaps she will want to draw the tree and seedpod beside the leaf. Reserve one blank page of your scrapbook beside each entry for discoveries on a winter's walk.

## BARK RUBBINGS

Take another walk in winter along the same route. This time take some sheets of typing paper and crayons in all shades of brown, black, and gray. Have the children stop at each of their "tree friends" and make a bark rubbing for their tree scrapbook. Tell the kids that trees are difficult to identify in winter without their leaves. Most people who know trees only observe their foliage. However, the bark of trees is really as different as the leaves. Making rubbings will help your children be able to identify the trees in this season, too.

Peel the wrappers off the crayons. (Do not throw them on the ground, but save them for your trash can.) Place a piece of typing paper on the tree trunk, and have the child rub with the side of a crayon which matches the color of the bark, until the paper has the clear imprint of the tree's "skin." These bark rubbings should be placed on the appropriate blank pages of your "Tree Friends" scrapbook. (See above.)

## ADOPT A TREE

Now that your kids are thoroughly aware of trees and can identify many natives of your area, have each child adopt a tree. It can be one you purchase and plant in your yard, a seedling you transplant from the woods, or a tree already growing somewhere. To adopt a pet tree, the child must study the variety in a tree book or ask in a tree nursery to learn its needs for fertilizer, water, insecticide, pruning, etc. Then on a regular basis the child should visit the tree and care for it.

This is especially meaningful if you can have the child actually plant the seedling and watch it grow through the years, as he himself grows. Try to find a young tree the same height as your child. Measure the child against the tree when he plants it, then every few months compare the measurements again. When he is grown and his children play beneath the tree, he will tell them how he planted it and cared for it. Teach the child that it is our responsibility to leave the places we go a little more beautiful than they were when we came.

A good way to practice what you preach about trees is to have living Christmas trees. After the holiday season, plant the Christmas tree outside.

## TREE TAG

When the children know the names of several different kinds of trees, go to a different place which has those varieties. Play "tree tag" to see if your children really learned from their study. Everyone gathers at a specific place, perhaps a picnic table. Have the "Tree Friends" scrapbook (see above) and authoritative tree guide book handy, but not open. Call out the name of a tree. The first child to tag the tree and return to you is "It" and can call out the name of the next tree.

## MY TREE PAINTINGS

Take an easel and your child's watercolor paint set outside. Set up in view of a large tree. Have the child paint the same tree in each season of the year. He will learn to observe not only the tree but also the seasonal changes in nature. Do not take a pencil for drawing the sketch first. Use acrylics or watercolors and a wide paintbrush so that trunk lines of the tree are bold and free.

In winter he will have the bare tree, with perhaps some berries or snow on it. Ask him to observe that snow is not just white, but reflects other colors, often appearing blue, pink, or gray. He will have fun trying to make the snow look real. For snow falling, he might get the brush drippy with paint and stand back and splatter it into the painting. Title the painting "My Tree" and hang it in your child's room for the season.

In the spring return with the easel and paints to the same spot and have the child paint the tree as it is in bud or bloom, or before the foliage is full. Perhaps a bird is building its nest in the tree, and he can add this to the picture. On this outing be sure to take along bits of colored yarn, string, and narrow strips of cloth. Have the child hang these on a low branch of his tree before he goes. Then each day return to the spot to see if a bird has used these to build a nest in the area.

For the child's summer painting, have him observe his winter and spring paintings before going to the tree. Tell him he must remember where the big branches are and paint them in lightly because they will not be clearly visible now when he looks at the tree in full foliage. Help him make his paint for the branches very thin so that he can add the leaves over it. While the skeleton of the painting is drying, tell the child to observe how many, many different shades of green and yellow are in the leaves. Now give the child a piece of a damp sponge, about two inches long. Have him dip it in turn into green, then yellow, then blue paints, each time blotting the sponge on the paper to paint leaves of that color on his tree. By overlapping these colors, thinned with water, he can mix them on the paper and achieve very natural looking foliage.

For your child's autumn painting, capture the tree at its peak of color. The child may want to use the sponge again, or have him try this very successful method: After painting the tree's skeleton branches again in thin paint, use full-strength red, orange, yellow, brown, and some dark green. Have the child dip a very small brush into one color, getting the paintbrush quite full but not drippy. He can dab spots of this color all over the tree, leaving paintbrush-size leaves of one color, with lots of space between. Clean the brush thoroughly, dip it into the next color, and repeat the action until both colors are spaced throughout the foliage area. Continue with other fall colors until the foliage is full on his tree.

## ARTIST'S SIGNATURE

Although you should teach your child not to harm trees, it would be a very special signature for your little artist to sign his tree, which has now become very important to him through the year of painting it. Take a knife and have him carve his initials into the tree. Then very carefully coat the initials with a tree preservative insecticide from your nursery. This teaches him to protect the tree. Keep the paintings of this tree for your child until he is grown. If you are lucky the tree will still be there with his initials for him to show his own child, who can repeat the same activity beneath the same tree.

## AT THE SEASHORE

If you live at the seashore or if it is possible for you to take a journey to the ocean, your children will be lucky, indeed. Many children have never seen the ocean. For them it is most important to get pictures and see films that show the mighty seas. With audiovisual aids in schools, museums, and libraries, every child should be informed about the ocean to some degree. Take the time to help your child learn from any means you can afford. See the chapter "Bath Time: the Highlight of the Day" for a toy ocean you can make from things you have in your kitchen. If you are able to visit the shore, here are some wonderful activities to help your children make the most of this fun learning experience.

## BEACH TAKE-ALONG

If your family is going to the seashore or lives near the ocean, this "take-along" for beach visits is a *must*. An ocean floor viewer is simple and inexpensive to make. When you use it you will want one for each member of the family, so you would be wise to make that many in the first place and avoid any arguments. Even Mom and Dad will want one. What you can see with it is fascinating!

Give your child a rectangular plastic dishpan and help him cut out a window in the center of the bottom, leaving a one-inch frame all around the flat part of the bottom. This can be done with an electric saw or with sturdy scissors. Cut or buy a piece of rigid, clear acrylic the size of the bottom of the dishpan, so that it overlaps the plastic frame you have left.

On the *outside* of the plastic frame remaining as the bottom of your dishpan, have the child paint a generous coat of rubber cement glue. Lay the clear acrylic against this so that it is glued on as the window pane. To be extra sure the viewing window stays secure under pressure from water, you can help your child drill holes and add bolts with nuts at two-inch intervals all around the window pane, if you have a drill and want to take this extra precaution. When complete, add another coat of rubber cement all around the edges of the acrylic and daub it into the screw holes, to be sure the crevices are waterproof.

When walking in the ocean, lay your plastic window directly on the surface of the water. You can peer into the dishpan and see clearly whatever is on the ocean floor. You can also observe some of the tiny particles that are floating in the water. You and your children will be amazed at what you can see!

If you don't want to make an ocean viewer, by all means give your kids a good pair of swim goggles to see the ocean floor.

## STUDYING SEA LIFE

While at the beach collect some sea water for later observation under a microscope. The numerous microscopic organisms which live in seawater are fascinating, but difficult to observe from just a drop of sea water. It is better to make a concentration by collecting the water in a ladies' stocking. Let it drip through until only about an inch of water remains in the hose. Pour this into a small, clean jar or pill bottle. Repeat the collection process until your jar is filled. You can look at this with a magnifying glass, but a microscope is much better to observe the minute community in which you swam. This opens an unbelievable world to you and your kids!

## NIGHT WALKERS

While at the seashore, by all means take a night walk on the beach with your children. Using a flashlight, spot the crabs and other creatures that come out at night.

## BUILDING CASTLES

Of course, your children will build a sand castle, but be well-prepared before you arrive at the beach. You don't need to purchase expensive sand molding equipment for your kids. Take several free implements which will make their castle fantastic instead of ordinary. For tall towers give your kids clean one-quart and half-gallon milk cartons and tall, slender potato chip cans with both ends removed (but use the plastic lid). Several clean, frozen-juice cans of varying sizes with both ends removed are also very useful for molding sand. Other items that make nice molds for your kids' sand castles are plastic butter tubs and yogurt cartons.

Also take several kitchen utensils to make attractive textures in the sand and for experimenting. Among those to try are a sifter, garlic press, potato masher, fork, spoon, blunt knife, and ice cube tray. Also take several long-handled spoons and large coffee cans for each family member. Save plastic tubs with a handle, such as peanut butter or ice cream containers, for sand buckets. Your kids' imaginations will go wild as they use these items you already have on hand to make the best sand castle ever.

## SHELL CRAFTS

Shell craft is lots of fun and a good way for your children to use those collections they brought back from the beach. When I was a youngster, I adored making things from shells. When leaving the shore from our once-a-year visit, I persuaded my father to take my large can full of newly-collected shells home with us so that I could continue my creations there. Without examining my collection, he placed it in the trunk of the car. We made the long, hot trip home and decided it was too late to unpack that night. The next day, when we opened the trunk to unload, we were attacked by a ferocious dead odor. I had failed to tell my father that the shells in my can still had the sea animals in them. Hundreds of little coquinas, whose butterfly shells I had intended to pry open later, had died in the trunk. We did everything to fumigate the car, which finally had to be traded because the odor was so horrible! Nature crafts can be expensive if you do not oversee your child!

### SHELL SCULPTURE

Using epoxy glue, your child can create the same kinds of shell sculpture you see for sale in all the beach shops. Have her observe these items for sale, and then help your child construct them at home. To wash shells without damaging your sink, have the child place the collection in a colander or strainer. Immerse the strainer in a larger pan of soapy water to which you have added a little bleach. The pan collects the sand so it can be thrown outside. Sun dry the shells for a day or two before beginning your creations. If she intends to make shell people, pipe cleaners are good for arms and legs. She can use felt-tipped markers for facial features.

### DECORATIVE STATIONERY

Your older children will enjoy gluing small shells in a design or picture on the front of a folded piece of stationery. It makes nice personalized stationery or an attractive picture to frame.

## DESK ORNAMENTS

Shell paperweights are simple. You might decorate a wooden box with glued-on shells. Or use a large shell to create a lamp by inserting a small socket cord that will hold a night-light bulb.

## SHELL JEWELRY

Your daughter can make fancy headbands or a set of barrettes for her hair by decorating inexpensive plastic ones with the shells and some tiny silk flowers or ribbons. Your little girls who enjoy playing "grown-up" and boys who enjoy playing "Indian" will love making and wearing shell jewelry. Purchase earring bases from the craft shop and let the youngsters have a jewelry making party so their friends can enjoy the fun. Necklaces can be made by stringing the shells, which have natural holes in them.

## SHELL MODELS

Children will treasure models of ships, airplanes, cars, and animals which they construct by gluing shells together.

## SHELL FLOWERS

A youngster who is creative may enjoy making shell flowers by gluing small shells together for the blossoms. The child can use a small piece of cardboard for a base and attach a sturdy floral wire to this for the stem. She can wrap the stem with floral tape. Using epoxy glue, she can glue the shells to the cardboard base and to each other to create the flowers, which can be tinted with food coloring or fabric dye, if she wishes. Lovely daisies, lilies, chrysanthemums, roses, etc., can be created in this manner.

## INSPIRING YOUNG HOSTS AND HOSTESSES

Help your teenager prepare a tasty seafood casserole and bake it in individual portions in large clam shells, to serve at a luncheon for friends. He or she can arrange a centerpiece of fresh or dried flowers in a large conch shell.

A party with a seashore theme will give your youngsters a chance to share their experiences and pictures with their friends.

## WINGED FRIENDS

How many birds can you identify? Purchase a pocket-size bird book with colored pictures. Take your children to the park for a picnic and pack the bird book in the picnic basket. As you eat, look for birds and find them in the book. Keep a bird notebook—a small spiral pad for each child. Ask him to keep it in his pocket whenever he goes around the neighborhood and to list any birds he sees. It is great to take on trips, because the birds in another area will not be the same. (For other bird activities see Index.)

In early spring, especially, have your children watch for birds from their window, identifying and writing down each one they see. In their bird books they should be encouraged to draw and color each one. Whenever they see that kind of bird again, they should list the date and place.

### COLLECT PICTURES

If you are studying birds, collect the U.S. stamps and postal cards which depict the official bird of each state. These are available at your Post Office, and make a beautiful and educational collection.

### BIRD CALLS

Order bird call recordings from:

National Audubon Society
950 Third Ave.
New York, NY 10022
(212) 546-9100

Listen together to learn to identify the birds you hear. Go for a family walk in the woods. One member of the family will be the leader, while all other members, blindfolded, join hands to walk slowly along a level path, or just sit quietly together. Listen to the bird calls and try to name the birds.

## NESTS TO FIND

Study pictures of birds' nests and eggs. This is another way to distinguish between the species. Look for nests in unusual places: a grassy meadow, reeds along a pond, a hole in a tree.

## HOUSES AND FEEDERS

Build birdhouses or bird feeders together. A very simple feeder can be made by cutting a hole in a plastic bottle, and tying the bottle by its handle to a tree limb. Get a hummingbird feeder also.

But if you live in a cold climate and begin to feed birds in winter, be aware that they become totally dependent on you for their existence. You must not fail to feed them for even one day, or they will die in the cold if they cannot find any other food. Another interesting and easy feeder is a large pinecone, spread with peanut butter and sprinkled with birdseed. Use your discarded Christmas tree as a tree for the birds. With bright-colored yarn, tie on it bits of suet from the butcher. As spring draws near, the yarn should be loosened so the birds can use it to build nests.

## OBSERVING NATURE

Your child can hone his senses and learn to detect things out-of-doors that most people never notice. Teach your youngster to observe and identify animals hidden in trees, or mushrooms beginning to sprout on the ground. He will have fun with these discoveries, and his naturalist skills will not only provide him many meaningful leisure hours during his adult life, but also could become a means of earning a living.

## ANIMAL TRACKS

When you are walking with your child outside, look for animal tracks to study. If you live in a city, finding tracks will be more of a challenge, but not impossible. Go to a park after a rainstorm and look for tracks of dogs, cats, birds, squirrels, or even people.

The youngster will have fun making animal footprints to

take home. He can do this by filling the tracks he finds with plaster of paris (from a craft or hardware store, or use patching plaster from a paint store.) When the plaster is set (in just a few minutes), he will have a terrific souvenir to show his friends and to study at home.

When he returns home have him trace the outline of the track onto cardboard or felt and cut it out. Then glue this to the bottom of the track to make it sturdier. He can make a collection of various tracks he finds through the years. Perhaps he will draw the animal and display his drawing with the tracks.

## WATCH WHERE YOU GO

While riding around town on a familiar route, ask your children to find a bush or tree that has bloomed since you last passed that way. Ask the kids to learn the name of one flower or shrub on each trip and to name it for you the next time you pass it. Later, in another place, ask them to identify a similar one by name. Have contests to see which child can name the most trees and flowers you pass.

## MYSTERIOUS MOON

What do you understand about the moon, the mystery we see nearly every night of our lives? Have you ever taken the time to read about it? Do so with your children. Use an encyclopedia simple enough for kids to comprehend. Learn how the moon controls tides, what the phases mean, how the moon affects weather and life on earth, about the lunar calendars and ancient superstitions. Learn about the discoveries made about the moon in our space age.

## OUR LIGHT SOURCES

To teach your children about the relationship of the earth, moon, and sun do this simple illustration at home. Have one family member hold a globe and turn it slowly on its axis. Explain that the rotating of the globe is the passing of a day and night. For the sun, another member holds a lamp with the shade removed. Note with the children that sometimes your state is on the lighted side of the globe and sometimes on the dark side of the globe as the earth turns.

Now have the child with the spinning globe (earth) begin to walk slowly around the one with the lamp (sun), to illustrate the passing of one year. Note with the kids that because the earth is tilted, sometimes one part of the earth is closer to the sun, and sometimes it is the other part of the earth that is closer. That makes the seasonal changes of hotter to colder times of the year.

Another child holds a round mirror on the opposite side of the earth from the sun and faces the mirror toward the globe and the sun, so that the lamp is fully reflected in the mirror and throws a round circle of light onto the globe. This represents the full moon. Tell your children the moon has no light of its own, but simply reflects the light of the sun.

This child holding the moon now begins to walk around the child holding the globe (earth), but not around the lamp (sun) He (moon) should keep the mirror in the same position as it was when he started so that as he moves around the globe the mirror still faces the lamp at all times. Observe with your children that the shape of the reflection of the light from the mirror (moon) to the globe (earth) changes as the moon passes around the earth, creating the phases of the moon, which vary every night. When the back of the mirror (moon) faces the globe (earth) and is between the lamp (sun) and globe (earth), it demonstrates the new moon phase of each lunar cycle. This experiment can be repeated as often as necessary for complete understanding.

## NATURE'S SOUNDS

Summer is a wonderful time to enjoy nature with your child. Take a blanket out and lie on the ground. Direct the youngster's attention to the sounds of nature. Ask how many different bird songs he hears. Try to find each bird. Ask him to identify other natural sounds: dogs, crickets, cicadas, etc. It is so important to teach children to listen for sounds that are not man-made. We are accustomed to tuning out many sounds. Your child will be fascinated and will find a pastime he can enjoy whenever he is alone outside.

## A TINY WORLD TO DISCOVER

While you are out in the park or on the lawn together, have the child lie with his ear on the ground and listen for the sound of insects in their little world. Look for the ones he hears. Get a book to study bees and ants. They are marvelously smart creatures. Studying both with your child is fascinating. If you live in an area with trees and flowers, perhaps your youngster will want to keep a beehive and collect honey. By all means, take a drive out of your city and watch for beehives in large white boxes. If you find any, feel free to stop and ask questions. Chances are, the beekeeper will enjoy showing your children about his hobby or business. Look in your yellow pages to try to find the nearest beekeeper.

If you are unable to locate bees, you will make other discoveries while driving in the country. Stop and inquire about things that interest you and your children. (See chapter on "Short Stops.")

If you live in a city and are unable to go to the country, consider purchasing an ant farm for your child's room. These are not expensive and can be purchased at pet stores. Your child will learn so much from watching the ants build their home and work together, all safely within the clear plastic container from which they cannot escape.

While out-of-doors drop a small piece of sweet food and watch the ants discover it. For a long while your child will be in awe watching the communication system and teamwork of the colony of little creatures, as they work together to store the bit of food.

Find a spiderweb and watch the female spider at work. Teach your child which spiders are poisonous. Others should be protected and appreciated, as they eat insect pests. Look for ladybugs, most helpful little creatures. Kids love watching ladybugs light on their arms and then fly away.

## NATURAL FINDS

As you take walks with your children, collect natural objects to keep in a special display at home. Perhaps they will find a hornet's nest (spray it with flying insect killer to be sure this is not a painful keepsake), a bird's eggs and nest (spray these for mites), driftwood, seashells, special rocks, seed pods, cones, etc. The items you collect will bring back fond memories each time your child looks at them. And these objects will provide the basis for a wonderful nature study on a rainy day when you can take the time to look up each one in a book to learn more about it. Your child may choose to study it with a microscope or magnifying glass, draw it, or photograph it. There are many ways that natural finds can be used to make home decorations as well.

## NATURE'S WARNINGS

Just before, during, and after a rain, have your children closely observe the sounds of nature and write down what they hear. The twitterings of birds and insects are a more accurate weather guide than your TV or radio weather forecaster. Children can learn to listen for the ways nature announces, "It's about to rain!" or "The rain is over for awhile." Other weather forecasters exist in nature. When it is about to rain, observe the way a spider spins his web or a cat licks her coat. Watch the pathway ants travel; listen for birds. You'll be surprised how many warnings of bad weather are all around us, and were here before the science of meteorology.

On a warm day when there is no lightning, take your child for a walk in the rain. It's a great way to help overcome fear of storms. Have the child notice how the flowers nod their heads, saying, "Thank you for the drink of water."

When the rain is over, go with your children for a barefoot squish in the mud and rinse feet in the puddles. Take a long stick and gently pick up the earthworms that have washed into the street. Have the kids return them to the grass so they won't die. Tell your children to observe how strong the delicate looking flowers are and how they are not usually damaged by the rain. Look for a rainbow. Observe the reflections in the drops of water on a blade of grass. Smell the fresh ozone odor that fills the air after a thunderstorm. Teach your child to observe nature with all his senses.

## THUNDER AND LIGHTNING

Whenever there is thunder or lightning it is wise to stay indoors. Have children clap their hands with the thunder and imagine that the noise could be "Indian drums" or the sounds of "angels bowling" or "Mother Nature clapping her hands." Talking about the friendly sound of the thunder will help overcome your child's fear.

Older children will be excited to learn that thunder is the explosion of the air molecules when heated suddenly by the lightning. If the child sees lightning, have him count, "one, one thousand, two, two thousand, three, three thousand," etc. until the thunder sounds. This tells approximately how far away the lightning is. For every 5,000 counted, the lightning is about a mile away. Explain that light travels faster than sound; therefore, we see lightning before we hear the sound of thunder. Our space-age kids can understand it well when you compare this to seeing an ultrasonic plane passing over before hearing its sound.

# CREATIVE OUTDOOR PLAY

**D**o your children often whine, "I'm bored!" and get underfoot? Do they continually loll in front of the TV? Why not disconnect the electronic monster and shoo them outside? If you are an inside person, the chances are your children are, too. For a wonderful gift to yourself and to them, force your family to develop the outdoor play habit. No matter what the weather or your neighborhood conditions, you will discover there is a marvelous world of fun right at your own back door.

If you are already an outside person, you know how much easier it is for a child to entertain himself outdoors. And since you are aware of the benefits of fresh air, you know your children are probably healthier, too. But read on to discover some different ideas for outdoor play and entertainment that you may not have considered. These are things your family can do together and that your children can continue to enjoy doing when Mom and Dad have to return to their chores.

## SAND PLAY

If you don't have a sandbox in your yard, it is one of the best items you can purchase or make. If you live in an apartment, try to persuade the manager to build a sandbox in the yard or on the roof. If that fails, perhaps you can find a corner of your porch in which to place a child's swimming pool filled with sand. It is worth the space and effort.

For a backyard box simply use four boards nailed together, with a triangular seat in each corner to make the box sturdy. You can find scrap lumber at building sites or warped pieces for free at a lumberyard. It is wise to sand them thoroughly (a belt sander is easiest if you have access to one) to prevent splintering. Paint the box if you wish. Or you might consider using an old tractor tire from the junkyard. It makes an excellent sandbox.

Because cats are a real menace to sandboxes, make your box so that it can be covered in some convenient way. One idea is to throw a tarp over it when not in use. Another way is to find two old screen doors and make your box the size to fit beneath them. A simple frame of chicken wire can be easily constructed. Or you might use a half-sheet of Masonite or thin plywood, which the children are taught to pull over the sandbox each time they leave it.

### SAND CREATIONS

Help your children to make castles with caves beneath, by packing wet sand around their feet, mounding it high, and then carefully removing their feet.

Other sand creations to build are: an alligator, a monster, a person, a whale, and block letters to spell your child's name. (See the chapter "Loving Nature Is Natural" for ideas on a sandy beach.)

On special days give the child glitter and spray paint to decorate his creation elaborately. This sounds like it would be horribly messy, but it is not. The spray paint should be used after the creation is finished. After it dries, the sand creation can be destroyed and raked and the paint and glitter will seem to disappear among the particles of sand.

## SANDY PARTY

When kids have the "blahs," a real way to cheer them is to have a "Very Merry Unbirthday Party" in the sandbox. Invite all the youngsters nearby to bring an "unbirthday present" to give each other. It must be gift wrapped, so it will be a "surprise" to open. (You might tell parents before the party that the gift is to be something within a given price range and for playing in the sand.)

When guests arrive, instruct them to make a giant "unbirthday cake," using all the sand in the sandbox. When the cake is complete, give them a can of shaving cream to ice the cake and sparklers for candles. Sing the song, "A Very Merry Unbirthday," which the children probably know from the Disney version of "Alice in Wonderland." (Supervise the burning of the sparklers and collect the used ones, so no one is injured.) Then the children unwrap their presents and play with them in the sand.

## SANDBOX CHEMISTRY

Show your child how to make a "real" volcano in a sand mountain. Form the mountain around a plastic cup and keep the mouth of the cup free of sand. When the mountain is complete, place a tablespoon of baking soda and some red food coloring in the cup. Give your child one-fourth cup of vinegar to pour into the mountain's cup. The volcano will boil over its angry foam, which is delightful, harmless and very dramatic. Have a good supply of soda and vinegar, because the kids will want to repeat this a number of times.

---

These ingredients are harmless if the children try to taste them, but warn the kids not to rub vinegar or soda in their eyes. It will sting. You may want to supervise this activity for preschoolers.

## SANDBOX CRAFTS

A craft your older child will enjoy in the sandbox is making sand castings in plaster or wax. The child should soak the sand thoroughly and pack it firmly. Then use a spoon and blunt knife to scoop out a hole in any shape desired. He can make the shape of an animal, a man, a house, or simply a geometric figure. The hole becomes the mold for the statue or candle the child will make.

When the scooping is completed, the child should pack the inside of the hole firmly all around, by mashing or patting it with his hand or a large spoon. Then help him fill the hole with plaster of paris (inexpensive at hardware stores) mixed according to directions.

If your child prefers to make a candle instead of a statue, he should prepare the hole as above. Then measure the depth of the hole. Insert a candle, which is the height of the hole, in the center. Then pour in melted paraffin to fill the hole instead of plaster. (Supervise the melting to avoid fire.)

When the medium is hardened remove it from the sand mold. The plaster figure or molded candle will still have sand clinging to it to give it a lovely texture. This makes a wonderful gift for anyone or a proud ornament for your child's room.

## PETS FOR FREE

Many unusual pets are right in your own yard, awaiting your child's interest. But teach your youngster to be kind. Grasshoppers, crickets, beetles, ladybugs, fireflies: each is of interest to your child, unless you act horrified by the creature. Then your child will also be afraid to touch and watch it. Make a study of insects in your family.

## TURTLE CONTESTS

Two turtles or terrapins caught on a summer day can be a source of great fun to your child. Placed beside each other, and coaxed with a little piece of tomato or strawberry several feet away, the turtles will race each other to the food.

If your youngster captures a small turtle, paint her initials on the shell before releasing the animal. Later search the same area to see if you can find the friend again, perhaps with a larger shell and your child's initials all stretched out!

## LIGHTNING BUGS

Catching lightning bugs is a favorite pastime of children on a summer's evening. But do not run the risk of severe injuries from broken glass jars. In this day of plastic, no child needs to run around with a glass container. We found that zipper plastic bags are great for collecting bugs. Make sure the bag is filled with air before closing it, and keep the bug inside only a little while until you can transfer him to your child's bug cage for his tiny insect zoo. (See below.)

## INSECT CAGES

Make several bug cages, so the captives can be fed and observed without harm and released when interest wanes. A cage is easy to make from a piece of window screen material (hardware cloth) cut in a twelve-inch square. Form a cylinder from the screen, taping it together with strapping tape. Encase the edges of the screen in strong tape, folded over to cover the sharp wires. Remove the top of two small tuna cans so that there are no sharp edges. Clean the cans well and use them for the ends of the bug cage. One can should be taped in place over the wire cylinder with strapping tape or duct tape. The other can should be removable to open the cage for cleaning, feeding, or adding new friends. Your child can watch the little pets through the screen.

## HARMFUL INSECTS

It is difficult for children to understand why some insects are harmful and must be destroyed through insecticides, while others are helpful and may be encouraged to stay in your yard. If your child has learned well the "be kind" lesson, it becomes traumatic if a harmful insect is captured for study. Perhaps books, which explain why the insect is a pest, may help the child understand. However, many insects that might be considered a pest in your home or yard may have an important place in the balance of nature—in the woods, or in a field. Help your child try to determine if the creature can be beneficial in any environment and take him to release it there, if possible. It will be a valuable lesson for your child not only in nature, but in being kind to all creatures. The child will relate to the consistency of your teaching.

## COLLECTIONS FOR SCIENCE PROJECTS

Although it is best to teach your child to be kind to every living creature, there are times he may be required in school to make a mounted collection of bugs or butterflies. To kill the insects in a humane way, cut a circle of heavy cardboard to fit exactly the inside of a wide-mouthed, pint glass jar, so that it has to be forced down into the jar. With an ice pick, punch several holes in the cardboard. Pour one inch of formaldehyde into the bottom of the jar. *(Caution: Formaldehyde is poison.)* Insert the cardboard. Lay the captive insect on the cardboard and close the jar lid tightly for a few minutes. The creature will die quickly and be preserved in good condition for your scientific display.

## WATCHING CREATURES

When all alone outdoors a child of any age can try this intriguing game. He should sit and look around him until he finds a creature to watch. It can be a cat or dog, a worm, a spider, or a bird. It does not matter what kind of animal or insect he chooses. A different one each time he plays would be even better.

The child must observe the animal for five minutes or more, very intently. He must watch each movement the animal makes and try to imitate it. Then the fun begins. Your child must try to "get inside the animal's mind." He must try to imagine just what the animal is thinking and feeling. Have your child pretend to be that animal for awhile. Later he should look up the animal in an encyclopedia or other reference book and read about its habits.

This is an especially good game to play with a child who has neglected or mistreated a pet. After trying to think as the animal thinks and feel as it feels, your child will be more considerate of the animal.

Ask the child to make up a story about the animal he has observed. It can be factual, simply relating what he has observed the animal doing and his own interpretation of its actions, based on his reading about the animal. Or it can be an imaginative story, personifying the animal and its relationships with its friends in a creative story in which your child becomes the animal. Have the child write the story or speak it into a tape recorder.

Read with your child outstanding children's animal literature, such as Beatrix Potter's stories of Peter Rabbit. Suggest to your youngster that the writer's creativity might have begun just as his did—with the imagination used in observing the animal.

This activity will become a favorite for times spent alone, and your children will learn a lot about a number of animals. Make trips to the library to get good animal stories and reference books. Encourage walks in the woods or at a farm to watch animals the child might not normally see. Ask him to sit beneath a tree and watch for birds in early morning or late afternoon. Have him lie in the grass to observe insects and other "creepy crawlies." He will develop greater awareness and creativity, which will follow him into adulthood.

## CATERPILLARS FOR LEARNING

Caterpillars are among the most fascinating of the "creepy crawlies" because your child can witness the magnificent transformation from caterpillar, to chrysalis and cocoon, to moth or butterfly. If your child captures a live caterpillar, look around carefully for the leaves it has been chewing. Put it into the cage (see above) and include his favorite leaves. Rain and dew clinging to the leaves provide needed moisture. Be sure to keep the leaf supply fresh, and after awhile your child may be rewarded by seeing a little cocoon attached to the side of the cage. If the caterpillar had enough food prior to spinning his cocoon you may be lucky enough to have a moth or butterfly emerge. This is a fascinating family learning experience.

## PET POLLIWOGS

Walk with your child beside a pond or other body of still water and search for tadpoles. These are easily caught with a large plastic bag. Put the polliwogs into a bowl with their own pond water and watch them grow into frogs. From your library get a book with illustrations of each stage and have the kids watch for the changes in the little creatures.

As the frogs grow, select one to let your child keep as a pet. Read the delightful story by Mark Twain, "The Notorious Jumping Frog of Calaveras County," and enjoy with your child the funny antics of "Daniel Webster," the frog who is trained to do wonderful feats.

Encourage several of your children's friends to adopt the other frogs and spend the summer teaching them tricks. As in the story, your kids, too, can have contests of leaps and jumps among their little pets. Don't fear the old wives' tale about warts being caused by frogs and toads. Dermatologists say it is simply not true.

You may think it all sounds too "yucky" to contemplate. But your children will think the little creatures are fascinating and will get hours and hours of entertainment and education from them, unless you teach the children that frogs are "creepy." Children have a marvelous, innate sense of wonder at all of nature unless it is, unfortunately, trained away. Help nourish this sense of awe and innocent pleasure in your children. Get books for them about their pet frogs and watch the contests excitedly. Then you can shudder secretly when you're alone!

## FUN FOR EVERYONE

Outdoor parties and games can be for just your family or for many people, depending on space and your budget. Encourage your children to plan and give different kinds of parties when they are outside with their friends. Here are some ideas that are really fun for everyone.

## BLOCK PARTY

Invite your neighbors to a block party. Block off the street from traffic for a few hours. (Get a permit if necessary in your city.) Have all the neighbors bring lawn chairs and their favorite dessert. You provide tea and paper products, or each family can bring their own.

If you have a tether ball, volleyball net, or croquet set, set them up for the kids. Or turn on the sprinkler for the youngsters to run through while the adults visit. It is fun to meet new neighbors and visit with old ones. In many places, a too busy life-style and the comfort of indoor air-conditioning have made us insulated from even those nearest us. The kids will love a festive block party. It will probably become a seasonal happening.

Repeat the event at Christmastime for caroling and building snowmen to decorate the street. Line the street with 32-ounce juice cans into which holes have been punched. Place a candle in each and light them all together, for the real Christmas spirit on your block.

If you live in an apartment, have an apartment party in the parking lot or a nearby park. You'll be glad to know your neighbors.

## BIRTHDAY PARTY

For a very special and inexpensive birthday party, have youngsters meet with their dads at a nearby park. Each child should bring a kite. Or you can make kites out of newspaper and two wooden dowels as part of the entertainment. Have kite-flying contests for prizes. When you are finished, roast weiners over a fire and make "s'mores" for the birthday cake, by stacking chocolate candy bars on top of graham crackers. Add to each a hot roasted marshmallow and a sandwich top of another graham cracker.

## LEARNING TO SKATE

As children are learning to skate, scraped knees can be prevented by letting them begin on a smooth carpet indoors.

You can purchase indoor skates from a Sears catalogue, or simply use regular skates with the wheels cleaned. They will not damage the indoor-outdoor kind of carpet. The next step is to skate on linoleum floors in a place where furniture has been removed for safety. When the kids have mastered that, they are ready to graduate to outdoor skating.

Find a smooth cement driveway or garage floor in the neighborhood and ask permission for your children to skate on it. Pad knees and elbows with soft pads which you can make from pieces of foam rubber encased in fabric, with elastic straps sewn on. You might want to put a helmet on careless or accident-prone youngsters, or even strap on a fanny pillow. These skating hours will be times of great fun.

## BALLOON CONTEST

A balloon contest is an innovation that really adept skaters will enjoy. Each skater wears balloons tied so that one trails about six inches behind each ankle. The tag game is played by each skater attempting to run over and pop the balloons of other players, while protecting his own.

## BIKE RALLY

What could be more fun on a pretty day than a bike rally! Help your children to organize a neighborhood one. It might become a weekly event and will provide hours of outdoor fun. But make this an unusual bike rally, one that provides a mental challenge as well as physical exercise.

Using a map of your area from your Chamber of Commerce, help your kids plan a route. Follow the route with them to determine ten points of interest about which they can write riddle clues. Then invite their friends to take the "Hunt-a-Clue Rally Route."

Before the rally write the riddle clues and place each one at a different place along the route. Each clue should lead to the next point of interest after the riddle is solved. Give the riders their first clue at your home, along with refreshments. Set a time limit for reporting back and show the outer limit boundaries on your map. Send the riders in pairs for more fun, at five-minute intervals.

Your own children, who already know the route, can set

up lemonade stops along the way or simply ride along for the fun. If the riders enjoy the rally, as they undoubtedly will, form a rally club and have each member take his turn planning the route on alternate weeks.

---

This game should never be played on a busy street. You might want to supervise the activity to be sure it is played safely.

---

### BIKE TAG

Another bicycle diversion is a form of tag. Several players decide who is "It" and give her a handkerchief with which to tag a player. While "It" counts to 50 with her eyes closed, others ride off in different directions. "It" proceeds to tag another player and pass the handkerchief to him. However, the second "It" hides the handkerchief in his pocket before setting off to tag another. Since no one knows who the second "It" is, the game becomes one of tricking and eluding each other.

### BIKE HIDE-AND-SEEK

Bicycle Hide-and-Seek is a sure cure for boredom on a pretty day. It is played the same way as on foot, only the bike must be hidden also. Perimeters should be set by the children before the game begins, so the players do not go so far that they become impossible to find.

### BIKE SCAVENGER HUNT

Have a bicycle scavenger hunt in which many different items must be found by team members within a given range and time limit. This game requires a little advance planning, because players should be given a map specifying the hunt's limits. Each player is also given a list of specific items to find.

These can be nature finds, or items which must be begged from homes. If the children must go to homes, warn them to stay in team groups and go only to houses of friends. The first team to get all the items wins.

## BICYCLE WAR

Bike war is fun. Players divide into teams of "Good Guys" and "Bad Guys" and are equipped with water guns. The object of the game is to catch and "shoot" each other. When a player is wet he is out of the game. This game must be limited to an empty parking lot or an area with short grass. It is not safe to play in the street.

## WATER SLIDES

For summertime fun, a homemade water slide is great entertainment for the neighborhood. Use a large sheet of heavy plastic from a hardware store or garden shop. These come in long, narrow rolls or in rectangular sheets. You might find some throwaway plastic sheets in trash bins behind computer or electronics stores. Place the plastic on a grassy area; a hillside is best, if you have one.

Any garden hose will suffice to flood the slide with water. However, the best way is to use a soaker hose or make one from an old piece of garden hose. Close one end with a stopper from a hardware store and poke holes intermittently along the hose. The fun could last all day, but your grass wouldn't appreciate it. Every few hours move the plastic to another area.

## STATUES

Did you play "Statues" as a child? Teach your children how. In a circular motion, one child swings another child by the arm and suddenly lets go. The second child must freeze in the position in which she lands and silently decide what kind of statue she represents in that position. The other players must guess what she is.

## MOTHER, MAY I?

"Mother, May I?" is a favorite nighttim
streetlight game your children should know. Playe
a row. One is "Mother" and stands away from the
other children. She tells each player, in turn, what k   of
step and how many to take toward her. The steps can be
giant-, baby-, or child-size. The player may not take the
steps, even after the order is given, until asking, "Mother,
may I?" Then "Mother" may say, "Yes," or "No," or "Take
them backward," or "sideways." If a player forgets to ask
"May I?" he must return to the starting line. The players try
to sneak closer to "Mother" when she is not looking. The
first player to reach "Mother" becomes the leader, and the
others begin again at the original line.

## STAR PARTY

Invite your neighborhood to attend a star-watching
party. An amateur astronomer with a telescope would be
happy to attend the party and let everyone observe and learn
about the heavens. Your children will never forget the event.
It's fun to build a fire and roast marshmallows and sing after
the observation period is over.

## CONSTELLATIONS

On a cold wintry night have a very special outing with
your family. Bundle up warmly and take blankets or sleeping
bags to an open field away from city lights. Have a private
star-watching party. Look for constellations which you have
studied before you left home. Take a flashlight and constellation chart along with you so that you can check to be
sure when you identify one correctly. Look for satellites,
falling stars, meteor showers, and the North Star.

If your children have difficulty making any sense out of
constellations, explain that the shepherds of old had nothing
to do but watch the stars at night and so they drew imaginary
pictures in the sky, naming the figures according to their
favorite stories. Your children can do the same thing. They
may see Mickey Mouse or Darth Vader outlined in the stars.

.iey rename a starry area, have them make note of the direction in the sky, the month, and the pattern of other stars near it. On a piece of blue construction paper, use gold stars to mark their new constellation. Each night the children can look for their starry friends and remember their locations, since they named them. (Look under "Stars" in the Index for other ideas.)

## PHOTOGRAPHY

Outdoors is the place to start your child in the hobby of photography. Purchase black and white film and a simple camera. Let him choose his subjects and do his own shooting. If you have a darkroom he will enjoy helping process his pictures. If not, he will eagerly await their return from the shop. He will learn as he looks at his photos how to achieve more artistic composition and become a progressively better photographer, especially if you read with him the instructions that come with the camera and on film boxes.

## LOOKING TO LEARN

Photographs are only one purpose of taking the camera on photography outings with your child. The camera is a tool that makes your child observe constantly what is around him. And it is also a tool for *selective observation*. The viewfinder limits what he can see and helps him to look at the world in a different way. If you have several lenses, you will open another world for your child. He can see small things in nature magnified or telescoped. He can bring faraway animals up close for study. With a fish-eye lens, he can see a broader view than with his eyes alone. He can use a macro lens to see the world of a tiny insect.

If you have no camera or extra lenses, you can still teach the child to look selectively at things. Cut a peephole in a piece of cardboard and have him peer through it, or make a "spy tube" from a cardboard cylinder from paper towels. (This can also be a tool to teach him better photographic composition if you do have a camera.)

For the child who is taught the love of nature, guns and hunting are abhorrent. To hunt with a camera is great sport in any season (*except* in hunting season, when you might be shot by a hunter with a gun). The trophies the photographer shoots can be framed for display and for his own self-esteem. If anyone can shoot an animal with a camera, he could have shot it with a gun. A camera requires even more skill than a gun, and a lot more sensitivity.

## OUTDOOR CRAFT

Find a small twig of about a quarter inch in diameter. Let the child use a paring knife, with your supervision, to strip off the bark and cut the stick to a length of about three inches. Flatten the stick on one side by shaving away some of the wood. The child can then carve his name in the flattened area. Use burned wooden match heads to char the carved letters and make them darker. With epoxy glue, attach a safety pin or brooch pin backing from the craft store. The child will wear his bar pin proudly.

## MAGNIFIERS

Give your child a microscope and a good set of field glasses for a birthday or Christmas gift. Help him learn how to use these educational tools for studying nature in a way not otherwise possible. Teach him to care for the tools properly so they will last a lifetime.

## DISTORTING SIGHTS

Your youngster will enjoy crafting his own make-shift magnifier lens. Fill a clear glass jar or bottle with water and tighten the lid securely. Have him hold the jar up and look through it, observing the way the images change when you look through it sideways or vertically. Together observe things through the air bubble in the bottle. Then pour half of the water out and look at objects through the water again. They are no longer distorted. Ask your child to try to figure out why. Read with him about convex and concave surfaces and about lenses. Your child will spend a long time just peering through the bottle of water. The distortions are similar to those in carnival house mirrors.

## CAMPING

Family camping has become one of the most popular leisure activities, surpassing boating, jogging, softball, tennis, skiing, hunting, golf, and many other sports. Has your family discovered this inexpensive and fun way to get to know each other better and have memorable outdoor experiences?

For the first trial run you might try camping in your own yard, or certainly in a very nearby place, so that you can return for necessary items and in order to keep packing of gear to a minimum.

There are so many places to camp, and most for only a modest fee. Because of the overcrowding of campsites in many state and federal forests, the Boy Scouts of America formed the Family Camping Association to provide extra camp facilities across the United States. Membership in the Association is ten dollars a year for the family and entitles members to use designated Boy Scout camps for family camping. Members receive the Council Camp Directory, a family camping equipment catalog, semiannual newsletter, etc. Send your fee to:

Family Camping Association
Boy Scouts of America
1325 Walnut Hill Lane
Irving, Texas 75038

Their phone number is (214) 580-2000

Another scouting aid for campers anywhere is also available through any Boy Scout office: *Introduction to Family Camping*. It gives many tips for things you should know and remember to pack.

When camping, remember to get a permit, if needed, to build a fire. Dispose of trash properly and leave your campsite as you would wish to find one for yourself. Take along water purification tablets if you will be in an area without safe water. Take plenty of insect repellent and sunscreen and some netting umbrellas to keep insects away from food. Pack an emergency medical supply kit, a first aid instruction booklet, matches, and flashlight.

If you are caught unprepared in a sudden downpour, you can improvise raincoats from inverted plastic trash bags. Cut a head-size hole for your face. Be sure to warn children of the danger of suffocation caused by wearing plastic over their heads without a hole for the face.

Your camera and some nature study books are as vital to every family outing as insect repellent and sunscreen. The fun of camping is not impaired but enhanced by incorporating learning. It all depends on how you present it!

# SHORT
# STOPS

As a leader of ten little fourth grade Cub Scouts, I thought I had the perfect idea for an easy, informative meeting that we would all enjoy. I had never viewed the behind-the-scenes workings of the Post Office, and I was curious. The Postmaster had recently suggested that I write a newspaper feature about children collecting stamps, and I thought it was a good idea. I would "kill two birds with one stone" and do my research while conducting my Scout meeting. Was I in for a surprise!

My ten little Scouts, individually, are sweet, intelligent boys who have been taught good behavior at home. They were excited about the field trip.

Before we drove to the Post Office, each boy wrote a postcard to himself, which the group considered a ridiculous idea. The boys kept exclaiming, "Whoever heard of writing yourself a letter?" as they laboriously filled out their own names and addresses.

In front of the Post Office the clerk in charge of our group met us. By coincidence, he was the father of a ten-year-old boy who was a friend of most of my Scouts. Perhaps he was aware of what lay ahead. I stood blissfully ignorant and happily anticipating the interesting experience for us all!

I informed Mr. Smith that each boy wanted to mail a card to himself and watch it go through all the processes. Mr. Smith gave me a slightly incredulous look and then nodded in agreement that it would be a wonderful learning experience. (Only *he* was aware that the learning would be mine alone!)

What I learned was *never, never, never* think you can predict the behavior of a group of ten-year-old boys! My little angels sweetly pushed their cards through the U.S. Mail slot marked "Local," walked in orderly fashion through the doorway to the inner sanctum, and turned instantly into ten demonic octopi! Mr. Smith spoke softly, describing each step of the mailroom as if nothing out of the ordinary were occurring. His job for the afternoon was to conduct the tour.

To my horror, two boys darted to the moving belt, which was passing packages onto trucks, and perched themselves on the conveyer, wondering aloud in which town they would arrive. As I moved swiftly to recapture them, I saw, out of the corner of my eye, three others dive head-first into a large open box behind Mr. Smith. Before I could get to those boys, who were in good spanking position, they emerged throwing hundreds of rubber bands into the air to rain onto the floor.

One little villain, who had been innocently standing beside Mr. Smith, excitedly yelled, "Hey, watch!" as he grabbed a rubber band and shot it across the mailroom. Instantly, nine other little demons began fighting their way into the box for rubber bands to shoot. I was ready to kill! I jerked a few Scout uniforms (the symbol of model boys!) out of the box, while warning the other menaces through clenched teeth, and at the same time trying to force a smile in the direction of Mr. Smith. To my amazement, he had moved obliviously on to the next stage of postal traffic, droning his knowledge to deaf ears.

The three culprits who had originated the rubber band horror were now examining the hand canceling machine and dutifully making it mark all over their *hands!* While retrieving them, I couldn't believe my eyes as I spied two other boys who had climbed to the top of a high cabinet and were shuffling through a stack of mail, spilling pieces as they searched. Two other villains were taking letters out of one postal box and putting them into another. I was fighting back my tears!

I looked helplessly at Mr. Smith to apologize and saw he was blindly going ahead with his tour description. By this time, one sweet child (*not* my own) had decided to have mercy on me and the U.S. Mail and was standing beside Mr. Smith, actually listening to him!

Miraculously, the hour finally ended. The mail in our town did get delivered the next day, and the boys did receive their own cards, which they had canceled themselves. But I have at least ten new wrinkles on my face, the battle scars of a field trip!

Now that you have been dutifully warned of what *can* occur, take the suggestions in this chapter at your own risk, and also to your family's delight and free entertainment! The learning experiences gained by exploring your own local places of interest will educate your children and family about your town, as well as about processes and productions that make up our world. A new appreciation of services and understanding of people will change the way your children think as they grow up. These field trips will give them first-hand understanding of many job possibilities they may want to consider.


## VISITING PUBLIC HELPERS

Should there ever be an emergency in your family, it would be most helpful if your children already had some visual concept of the emergency helpers and public officials who provide services in your town. It is also comforting to a child to know what these public service places look like. When you are looking for family entertainment and an hour or two away from home together, take your family on these field trips around your own town.


### FIRE STATION

Most little children beg to go to the fire department to see the big trucks. If your child's class does not take this tour, by all means take your family, or ask permission to bring a few children for your child's birthday party. Firemen are more than willing to show the emergency equipment and the fire-house, and to give fire prevention literature. Ask if your local station has a fire prevention film your group can see. Several are available and are quite fascinating. If you go during National Fire Prevention Week (the second week of October), your children might receive free toy fire hats or coloring books.

## POLICE STATION

At your local police station, besides seeing the interesting facility, the children might have the opportunity to be fingerprinted. These fingerprints are a valuable item that should be stored in your safest place for identification of your child in case of loss or kidnapping. Ask to see the room of stolen bicycles. Perhaps your child will recognize one a friend has lost. You might take your child's bicycle to be marked with proper police identification, in case it is ever stolen. This is a free service at most stations.

Ask the officer to show older children the display of forbidden drug paraphernalia and talk to them about drug abuse. Just before your teen gets his driver's license, take the tour of the police station with him and request to see films or slides of automobile accidents. A few gory pictures are worth a thousand words of warning about wearing seat belts or not driving after drinking alcoholic beverages.

If you see any people in jail, talk afterward to your children about these people having made wrong choices and lost their freedom. Ask the officers if there are items which your family can provide to show compassion for those in prison, perhaps Bibles, magazines, or candy. Find out what is permitted and help your children collect a few of these items to give to attendants in charge of distribution.

Tell your children that you are proud of them when they do right and that it would break your heart if they ever committed a crime and had to be locked away. Tell them also that there is never anything that could make you stop loving them. Unconditional love is the greatest gift you can give your children.

## TOUR A HOSPITAL

Before any member of your family faces a hospital stay, take the children on a tour of the facility to reduce anxiety, or take the tour just for information. Someday, if you need the emergency room, the hospital will already be familiar to the child.

Ask that your tour include the pediatric section and, if possible, the nursery with its newborn babies. Many hospitals now offer to children educational presentations that include X rays and models of parts of the body, measuring the child, weighing him, and giving health tips and booklets.

When you return home you can reinforce some of the things your child has learned. To help her understand more about her body and that hospitals are places where people go when their bodies are not functioning properly, have her lie on a large sheet of paper. Draw around her with a felt-tipped marker, making a life size "Me Poster." Help her to draw in her heart, lungs, stomach, brain, etc.

Show her pictures in the encyclopedia of how she looks inside. Let her ask questions and record her own vital statistics and count her pulse for one minute. Take her temperature and record it, showing her how to read a thermometer and explaining about normal body temperature.

## CITY SERVICES

Have you ever seen the local water purification or sewer plant, or your city dump? These are tours your family would find very informative.

## PUBLIC TRANSPORTATION

Has your family ridden on a train or bus or flown on a plane? If the pocketbook permits, it would be a marvelous part of your children's education to ride on every type of public conveyance while growing up. If you cannot afford the more expensive means of transportation, you can ride on a city bus or subway, if available, and take a brief taxi ride, just for the experience. By all means, read about different types of transportation and request an official tour of the local transport facilities. It is not enough just to go to an airport to watch the planes land. Ask for the official tour. You will see things you could not see otherwise, and you will come away much more informed.

## MEDIA SERVICES

Your family should understand about media services. Take your children to see the local radio and TV stations and newspaper offices. If you request the official tour and explain that your intent is to help your group be as informed as possible, you might be permitted to watch the production of a show or even to have your group taped, whether for airing or just for fun. Perhaps your children will be allowed to go into the sound room and have a voice test. The newspaper office may have paper roll ends to give your children for their art projects. You might even enlist your youngster for a job as a newspaper carrier.

## GOVERNMENT OFFICES

What do you know about your government offices? Take your children with you when you pay for a car license or taxes. Ask for a tour of the building and any educational material. Ask what programs and services are available for children.

## COURTROOM

What about watching a trial? This is a wonderful way for your children to learn about due process of law. Find out when new citizens are being naturalized. Before going to the impressive ceremony, read to your children the Bill of Rights of our Constitution and explain that these new citizens will now be afforded all these rights into which your children were probably born. Your family will never forget the experience, nor will the Pledge of Allegiance to the flag ever be more meaningful.

## FIELD TRIPS FOR FUN

While some excursions are specifically for learning, as those mentioned above, others are for sheer family fun. But a lot of learning occurs secondarily on the short stops listed in this section. Take as many of these little trips as you can with your children. You will also think of others around your area.

## CITY TO COUNTRY

Do you live in a city? Have your children ever seen a real farm? It is not as impossible as you may think. Call the County Extension Agency, listed in your telephone book under the county name, and ask if they could arrange for you to visit a nearby farm.

If you are driving in the country, stop at a country store and explain that your children would like to visit a farm. The store owner may even know a farmer who has children the ages of yours and would delight in showing some city kids the wonders of country life: cows, chickens, horses, pigs, grain, a vegetable garden, and a tractor. In return, your children may find some new pen pals whom they can entertain later in the city.

## LEARNING ABOUT YOUR OWN LOCALE

If you live in a farming community, have you ever taken your children to the local granary? It is most interesting to visit in the fall when grain is being weighed for storage and sale. Or have your children been to a cattle auction, or sale of other animals? Find out which day is best to visit and go for a fascinating afternoon. Learn when the county fair and exhibition are and go to see the livestock shows and competition. Many children compete for prizes, exhibiting animals they have raised by themselves. Who knows? Your children may suddenly decide on a new hobby.

## BE A TOURIST IN YOUR TOWN

What do you go to see in other towns when you are a tourist? Museums, art galleries, historic sites, and cathedrals. How many of your local ones have you seen? Take your children on a "vacation at home" and visit all the places tourists see when they come to your area. Call your local Chamber of Commerce for the list, locations, fees, and time schedules. It's fun to see your hometown from an outsider's point of view. The children will bring home many pamphlets to decorate their bulletin boards.

## STARS AND SPACE

Is there a planetarium or space center nearby? This should be a point of interest to visit frequently. Augment the visits with books on the program's subject. For instance, if the planetarium presentation features summer skies, get a book on the same topic so the child can further enhance his new knowledge.

## PET STORE

Take your children frequently to the local pet stores. Unless you plan to purchase a pet, make sure the youngsters understand before you go that this is only a *looking* visit. Take time to pet the animals, to talk to the birds, to learn about the fish. If you cannot have pets at home, regular visits to the pet store are a perfect substitute. Your older children might volunteer to help the owner clean cages in order to spend more time and get to touch the animals more. If you are able to purchase a pet, get a small book about the particular kind of animal so that your child learns everything he can about his new pet and cares for it properly.

## VETERINARIAN

If you have a pet, a visit to a veterinarian may not be an unusual trip. However, you may never have thought to take your children with you. If you have no pet, visiting a vet's office is an eye-opening experience. Take them to see where pets are boarded. Let the kids watch a dog receiving his shots, being groomed, or being dipped for fleas. Ask also to see the area for large animal care; it is usually done in an area away from small pet care.

Go to the local ASPCA, too. But beware, you may come home with an extra mouth to feed!

## ANIMAL PARKS

Of course, if you have a local zoo the children have wanted to frequent it. But perhaps you have never thought of going for a field trip to a park where there are a few ducks on the pond. Take a bag of stale bread to feed them, and don't forget your camera. You'll get some priceless pictures at these pet places.

## PLACES THAT EXPAND LITTLE MINDS

As your children grow, they will think of what they want to be when they grow up. These ideas change from month to month and year to year. Listen to the roles your child declares he wants to play and take him to see that kind of working person on the job. Use any opportunities available to you to expand the growing mind of your child. Introduce him to jobs and workplaces he has never heard of. Look around your town and select places you would also like to see. Most companies welcome local interest, as long as you teach your children to be considerate and take proper precautions if the place visited has potential dangers.

### FACTORIES

Is there a factory in your town? No matter where you live, you can find some kind of manufacturing plant to take your children to see. Perhaps it may be a bottling company, a clothing manufacturer, a cannery, a large bakery, a paper mill, or a car manufacturer. If it is permitted, take your family to view the production of whatever is made in your town. You will become more informed about your community and your children will not take for granted the products they use. You might even be lucky enough to leave with some free samples or be able to purchase products wholesale at the company store.

### CONSTRUCTION SITES

What little boy doesn't adore hammering nails into wood or building with blocks? What little girl doesn't draw her dream house of the future? Have you ever taken the children to see how house plans are drawn? Visit a realtor or an architectural firm. Look at blueprints and house models. Go to a cabinet shop and see how cabinets are made. Your kids will be able to take home scraps that are normally discarded.

Visit a construction site of a large public building. Ask to see the model. Then have the children notice, as the building progresses over the weeks and months, how it grows to look like the model. Tour a house under construction and retour it at each stage of progress. The children will be fascinated to watch it go from foundation to painted house. Talk with the workmen and encourage your children to ask a few questions about how they do their jobs.

## GARAGE

Have you ever watched a car being repaired? Do you know what is under the hood of your own car or how to change a tire? Your little ones can learn many things by observation and may be able to tell you what is wrong the next time you have car trouble. Take the time to make a trip to a friendly garage where the mechanic is willing to take a few minutes to explain to inquisitive children what he is doing. Try to find a small, private garage at the home of a semiretired person for this kind of education.

If you're lucky, the mechanic might be willing to become a surrogate grandfather and teach your teenager all about car care in the afternoons or on weekends. This could be a source of valuable companionship and sharing for both.

## HIGHER-LEARNING FACILITIES

Is there a college, university, or technical school in your area? Telephone to ask which parts of the facility might be of particular interest to children. Many schools offer programs for area youngsters. Especially interesting may be the biology department, with its collection of animals. But be prepared for a surprise. When we visited our college biology department, to my dismay, they were giving away white mice. We came home with two of them and an ecstatic six-year-old.

The computer department of the college may permit your children to work a computer, and the only thing you might bring home from there is a collection of printouts!

Visit the art department to see student exhibits and perhaps a museum, or view a collection on display. If you do nothing else, at least walk through the campus on a Sunday afternoon and note the buildings. Many colleges have free or nominal film showings, plays, dramatic productions, lectures, and concerts. Find out about these and ask if your family is permitted to attend. You may discover that many forms of information and entertainment are available there, free for the asking. (See the "Hooking the New Reader" chapter for ideas about visiting the library.)

## ARTISTS' WORKSHOPS

Every town has its local artists, whether they be musicians, painters, sculptors, carvers, potters, or other types. Each is proud of his accomplishments and would love the opportunity to show his endeavors to your family. Many will also be happy to describe the steps and demonstrate their art to interested, well-behaved children. Your child may fall in love with the art form and decide to take lessons or dabble in the hobby at home. If you are able to afford to purchase something from the artist, by all means do so, in order to show your appreciation of his achievements and for his time spent with you. It will be a source of pride and inspiration to your child when he returns home with it to display.

## CRAFTSPEOPLE

A craft shop is a marvelous place to spend an afternoon with your children, if you have a few dollars to spare. It is nearly impossible to get out of a craft shop without the children purchasing something.

Watch your newspaper for arts and crafts demonstrations. Many are free and encourage kids to watch or try.

## OTHER LOCAL INTERESTS

Other ideas you may never have considered are a boat shop, welder's shop (protect your eyes), taxidermist, electronic repair shop, cobbler, army surplus store, junk shop, junkyard, shipyard and dock, and Armed Forces Reserve centers.

## CHURCH SERVICES

Weekends are often the best days to take family field trips. Have you visited every different kind of worship center in your town? It is a most interesting and enlightening experience, particularly if you spend the week reading about the beliefs of a particular denomination or religion. What better way could you educate your children to be tolerant of others' beliefs?

## THE WORKPLACE

Perhaps the most important visit your child can make is to the parents' places of work. Many youngsters have no idea what is meant when they say, "Mom's at work," or "Dad's at the office." If you can arrange to have the child come for a brief visit during working hours so he can get a real idea of what his parents do all day, so much the better. If not, obtain permission to bring him after-hours so that the child has a good mental picture of where his parents are each day.

Likewise, it is just as important for you to visit your child's school. He will be proud to conduct you on a tour and introduce you to his teachers and principal. You should do this at least once during each school year. It's ideal if you can arrive a few minutes before classes end so that you can see your child at work and then go for the tour.

As you drive around your town, watch for opportunities for an interesting field trip for your family. Always call ahead to make sure you won't be intruding. Prepare your children for what they will see. Caution them about necessary safety measures. Remind them to be courteous and on their best behavior. Follow up with a thank-you note, and family reading and discussion of what everyone has learned and seen.

# ON THE GO!

I n this chapter are many ideas which will make trips or mere errands around town more enjoyable for everyone. During our first five years as parents, we traveled with our children over 250,000 miles—the equivalent of going around the world ten times! These trips included short jaunts to a farm, camping trips, two-thousand-mile car trips to see grandparents, and flying to six foreign countries. During this time, we gathered a lot of tips on traveling with kids!

Now you may think my first and only tip should be, "Leave the kids at home!" I will readily admit that traveling without children is far easier and less expensive (no matter *what* baby-sitters cost!). But trips together bond a family, providing leisure hours to enjoy each other. You will collect warm memories and funny stories which will enrich your and your children's lives.

My husband and I laughingly remember how awesome packing the car was for that first visit to Gramma's house! New parents feel compelled to take everything the baby owns, from bathtub to high chair. We succeeded in cramming it *all* into our station wagon. We arranged the baby's car bed first and then fit the diaper bag, diaper pail, toys, infant tub, folded high chair, and suitcases around it. We even placed a room thermometer on the seat to be sure we maintained the perfect atmospheric temperature.

Fortunately, the maid was not quite finished cleaning the house when we were ready to leave. She agreed to lock up behind us.

We were worn out from the stress of packing everything and were quite relieved that the baby had slept through it all instead of screaming, as many babies do amid tension. Checking to make sure we hadn't forgotten one thing our little one might need, we sighed a tired, "Whew!" as we finally got ourselves into the car and drove away. We had driven to the end of the block when my husband looked into the rearview mirror and saw the maid frantically waving the broom and calling to us. We returned to ask what was the matter. Minnie breathlessly exclaimed, "You forgot the baby!"

In our family we also love to tell another funny travel experience of our first years traveling with children. When my husband informed me that we were to spend a month in Australia on business, I panicked! Although we never even considered leaving our twenty-month-old daughter behind, she wasn't "potty trained!" Even if disposable diapers had been popular then (which they were not), what airplane could hold a month's supply? And disposable paper products of any kind are not readily available in other countries, nor are launderettes! We immediately began a crash course in toilet schooling. Fortunately, she graduated with honors before our departure deadline.

However, that presented another traveler's problem: public (and even worse, *foreign*) toilet seats! I solved this by purchasing a "junior toilet seat," a rigid white plastic ring just slightly smaller than a normal toilet seat. Not being able to pack this "necessity," I dutifully wore it on my arm with my purse in taxi, train, and bus, and through every airport. Such are the sacrifices of motherhood!

After a week of traveling, I had become unconscious of the item I was lugging around. My husband's parents and teenage sister met us at the Brisbane Airport. I was puzzled by their rather cool greeting. A few minutes later, as we walked through the busy corridors to get our luggage, I heard

---

### Travel Toilet Seats

Purchase a package of disposable paper toilet seat covers to keep with you when traveling with children. For very small children you might want to purchase a fold-up toilet ring which can be stored in a plastic zipper bag in your purse or the car glove compartment. Keep a small bottle of rubbing alcohol with it for sterilizing the ring.

---

behind me the adamant stage whisper of my young sister-in-law, "I don't care if they *are* family. I will *not* walk with her while she has that thing on her arm!"

## TRAVEL WITH BABY

When traveling with a baby don't take everything you own. You can improvise, borrow, or purchase nearly anything you might need. The fewer things you have to keep up with, the freer your hands are for the children, and the more enjoyable the trip is for everyone. Babies who are taken frequently to different environments quickly learn to sleep anywhere and to be content with watching the activities in new places and among different people. The secret of a happy baby, while traveling or at home, is for Mom and Dad to be relaxed.

### BABY'S MEALS

During a trip, baby will be just as content and well-nourished eating all fruit at one meal, all vegetables at another meal, only meat at another. *You* might not want a meal of just carrots, but baby will not know the difference! This eliminates the need for refrigeration or warming. Feed him directly from the jar, throw away the empty jar or small unused portion, and clean the spoon with rubbing alcohol on a paper towel.

### EASY REACH

Babies old enough to be bored in a car will enjoy having a basket of toys tied to the car seat. (A soft, woven-plastic bicycle basket works particularly well.) Select his favorite toys and tie them to the basket, using strips of half-inch-wide elastic (safer than string). He will play happily for long periods and will quickly learn that he can retrieve a dropped toy by pulling the elastic. Just as in high chair play (see "Kitchen Kapers" chapter), he will delight himself by making a game of throwing his toys down and tugging them back up.

## BLESSED PEACE

A lost pacifier can cause a terrible roar from a baby already tired from riding. Prevent this by pulling a cloth diaper or napkin through the hole in the pacifier handle. This is safer than tying the pacifier to a ribbon around baby's neck. With this cloth in it, a lost pacifier will usually land in baby's lap. He quickly learns to put it back into his mouth by himself. If the pacifier does hit the floor, it usually lands on top of the cloth and remains clean. And you always have a burp cloth or spare diaper there if you need it!

## SLEEPY BABY

After making sure that he has on a clean diaper and is not hungry or ill, resist the temptation to take a fussy baby out of his carseat. He will soon learn that crying does not yield freedom and will resort to sleeping instead.

## TEACHING TRAVEL SAFETY

Automobile accidents present a risk more than twice as great as *any* other cause of death in children. Perhaps you recognize the danger and, therefore, require your kids to wear seat belts when you go out of town. But are you aware that most car accidents involving children occur within city limits and at speeds under 30 miles per hour? More than ninety percent of all injuries and deaths of children in car accidents would have been prevented by simply taking a moment to fasten the seat belt.

Any parent who has tried to get a little Free Spirit into a car seat or seat belt and keep him there, while maneuvering through heavy traffic with the child screaming, can tell the safety authorities that this is more easily said than done!

Small children who are accustomed to freedom when riding in the car will fuss and refuse to wear seat belts. But *if* you are firm and unyielding in your enforcement of the seat belt rule, their crying will persist for only a few trips. However, if you give in to their complaints once, they just learn to cry louder and longer until you give in again. And if you give in

---

### Baby Safety In the Car

• Infants and young children under four must *always* be secured properly in approved baby restraint devices (baby car seats).

• If baby needs to rest or be changed, stop the car in a safe place and let the whole family take a break.

• Any baby restraint device which meets approved safety standards will protect your baby *only* if you install and use it according to manufacturer's directions.

• For information about the safety of car seats, send a self-addressed, stamped, business-size (#10) envelope and 50¢. Request the *Shopping Guide for Car Seats:*

    National Passenger Safety Association
    P.O. Box 65616
    Washington, D.C. 20035
    (202) 429-0515

• Begin the practice of using the proper safety device when you bring the new baby home from the hospital. Then he will never know there is any other way to ride.

• In many cities, pediatricians, law enforcement agencies, libraries, hospitals, and PTAs have safety seats available for loan or nominal rental. If no group in your town has a car seat loan program, suggest the idea to a church or civic organization.

and allow them freedom in the car, *your* crying and regret may last a lifetime.

Here are some ways to make the safety habit a game instead of an ordeal when you are first beginning to enforce the use of proper safety restraints in the car.

---

### When To Use Seat Belts

A child over four years or forty pounds should ride on the seat of the car with the automobile seat belt snugly secured at all times. A child over four feet, ten inches tall should wear the shoulder strap also.

---

## SAFETY WARDEN

Teach your children that the car will *not* start until everyone is buckled up. Set the example by buckling your seat belt, too. Print "Safety Warden" on a circle of cardboard or on a stick-on name tag. Let children take turns wearing it, with the responsibility of telling the driver when everyone is safely buckled so the car can start.

## SEAT BELT INITIATION

If you have never used seat belts on a routine basis in your car or car pool, plan a special outing. About fifteen minutes before leaving, gather the children and tell them where you are going, encouraging their excitement and enthusiasm. Ask, "How many of you are big enough to fasten your own car seat belt?" With a show of hands, encourage the children to talk about the reasons to wear seat belts. Then announce that this outing is very special because it is the formal initiation of the seat belt rule for your car. State that whoever wants to wear a seat belt may ride with you. Any who object must stay at home.

Then have a contest to see which child can seat himself in the car and properly adjust and fasten his seat belt first. Offer a prize for the contest winner.

---

### Time To Buckle Up

Before leaving on your car pool run, make sure all seat belts are in place, not behind the seat. Plan ten extra minutes in your schedule to allow for the delays of little ones buckling up. This prevents your own frustration and prevents the temptation not to take the time because you are late.

---

## TRAP MR. SEAT BELT

If you repeatedly have the problem of the seat belts sliding behind the seat, purchase (at an auto parts store) some glue that is compatible for foam rubber and fabric and is heat-resistant, to withstand summer temperatures in a car parked in the sun.

With your children, play a game of "Trap Mr. Seat Belt." Ask the kids to pretend they are sheriffs trying to apprehend Mr. Seat Belt, who is lazy and tries not to do his job. As sheriffs, the kids are to locate Mr. Seat Belt's hands and put special handcuffs on them, so that he cannot shirk his duties by hiding his hands again.

While the children dig behind the seat for the lost seat belt ends, cut three-by-four-inch rectangles from two-inch-thick foam rubber. Instruct the kids to glue a rectangle of foam to both parts of the seat belt. On retractable belts the foam should be glued near the buckle. On adjustable seat belts, the foam piece must be glued to the end of the adjustable strap. The foam rubber will prevent the belts from slipping behind the seat.

You can hand sew the foam rubber in place, using a large needle and dental floss instead of thread, if you prefer not to purchase the glue. Wear a thimble to help push the needle through.

## IDENTIFY WRITE

Before any outing have your child print his name and your name, with complete address and phone number, and attach this to the inside of a garment which he will not be taking off (not a jacket). If garments are loose-fitting and have no pockets, write with permanent ink and place the I.D. in the child's shoe. Or write this information on the inside of the tongue of each shoe with permanent ink.

If you are taking a trip, whether or not you are traveling with the child, it is a good idea to include also your destination and the contact information for the nearest relative. The child can print this information in permanent ink (laundry marker) on iron-on interfacing and iron it to the inside of his shirt. You can iron this again when you return home, and remove the interfacing while it is hot.

When you are helping your child prepare his identification, talk to him about what he would do if he were separated from you and could not find you. (See ideas in the chapter "If I Were You.") Talk in nonthreatening ways about the importance of proper identification and show him your driver's license, telling him that you always have this with you when you are away from home. If your child has any medical alert conditions, be sure the information is included on the I.D.

## NO NAMES, PLEASE

Teach your children that in public places they should not wear items with their names visible . . . on T-shirts, or belts, etc. Knowing the name could give an ill-intended stranger an advantage over a trusting child. When packing for a trip talk to your children about which shirts or belts are for home wear and which ones are OK for wearing in public or on trips. With a few reminders, they will be able to make proper selections for trips or outings by themselves.

## HELPFUL HANDIES

Use a large plastic trash bag to stow emergency supplies under the seat of the car. The bag itself can be used as a picnic mat, or protective seat cover for bleachers or the ground, or used as an emergency raincoat by cutting a large hole for the face. (Be sure to caution children never to put a plastic bag over their faces.) Have your children help you think of emergency things your family might need to place in this bag. You might include a diaper, pacifier in a protective plastic zipper bag, extra underwear for preschoolers, washcloth and small bottle of rubbing alcohol (for cleaning hands or sterilizing pacifier), hair brush, candy mints and gum, folding scissors, masking tape (great for emergency hems!), bandages, paper clips, rubber bands, pen and paper, book (for parents who spend hours waiting in the car for children) needle and thread, folding cup, screwdriver, flashlight, and collapsible umbrella.

## ENTERTAINING CHILDREN IN THE CAR

You can adapt all of these tips to be used any time you are away from your child's normal environment or any time the child is required to sit still for long periods. Remember as you read that these ideas are for any trip you take, whether going across the country to see grandparents for the summer or just around the corner to get a loaf of bread.

### MAKE A HAPPY KIT

Children who are too small to see out of the car windows quickly tire of riding. To make trips and errands more fun for everyone, help each young child prepare a Happy Kit to keep himself entertained while riding. He will need a surface on which to play and a way to store all his car entertainment. There are several different ways you might help kids make Happy Kits.

Get a sturdy cardboard box and remove the flaps. Turn it upside down and cut out a semicircle on the long sides of the box for leg room. This will serve as a car play table across your child's lap. Your child can help by fitting it over his lap and advising you where to recut to make it fit just right. Children can decorate the box by drawing pictures on it or cutting some from magazines or catalogues. Or you can help them cover the box with adhesive-backed vinyl or vinyl wallpaper in a youngster's choice of design. (Ask your wallpaper dealer for odd lots or leftover rolls, which are usually very nominally priced.)

Make a drawstring cloth bag for your child to fill with some favorite toys that he is willing to keep in the car. Store the toy bag in the box while not in use.

Another simple play table for the car is a lap tray with

legs. A metal one works best because magnetic toys will
adhere to it.

A child's metal lunch box might be used to store the toys
and for magnetic play. It could also serve as a small table
surface in the car. This makes an ideal Happy Kit because
your child can easily carry it into a restaurant or doctor's
office, where he might need entertainment while waiting.

A covered metal cake pan with a slide-on lid also makes
a good Happy Kit. These make wonderful birthday or Christmas gifts for children or grandchildren.

---

### Select Travel Toys

Carefully select toys that will be safe during car motion. They
should promote quiet activity, have long interest appeal, and
have no sharp edges or tiny parts that could be swallowed or
lost.

---

Help your child select new or old toys to fill his Happy
Kit, with the agreement that whatever he chooses to place in
the kit will remain there, for travel use only. Encourage the
child to choose items with long interest appeal and which
lend themselves to more than one kind of activity.

Some toys most young children will enjoy in the car are:
a coloring book; washable crayons (these are plastic and
won't melt as easily as wax crayons); magnets and magnetic
letters and figures; small cars; little plastic animals and people; an old deck of cards; a magazine; glue stick; blank spiral
notebook; colored pipe cleaners; clay in a zipper sandwich
bag (make your own from the recipe in the "Kitchen Kapers"
chapter); a punch out sticker book; paint-with-water book
and cotton swabs to use for paintbrushes; stickers (Easter or
Christmas seals work great); bubble liquid; small doll with
long hair, little brush, comb, and mirror; tape; blank paper;
small plastic magnifier; lacing cards; small books; ka-
leidoscope; washable felt-tipped markers.

---

### Plan For Cleanups

Be sure to include premoistened towelettes. For success with this kit permit only one toy to be taken out at a time.

---

Your children will be familiar with the traditional use of each of these items and will play happily for long periods. But, on a long trip, there comes a time when they tire of the toys and become bored. In this section you will find some innovations you can suggest as new ways to play with things that have had only limited traditional use.

---

### Sick Kids, Too

Many ideas in this travel chapter are excellent activities to do with a child who is confined to bed or hospitalized for injury or illness. They are also good activities for pre-nap time, or to keep the child who has grown too old for "nap time" quietly amused during a rest time.

---

## MAGAZINES ARE FUN

Every parent knows a child can use a magazine as a book to look at the pictures. But when he has tired of this, print a word for the child to locate ten times in the magazine. This is a great way to encourage learning to read, and will occupy him for a long while. Read some of the stories to him. Later suggest that he tear out pictures to glue or tape into a spiral notebook to tell a story about his family. You don't have to have children's magazines for these activities; discarded adult magazines serve as well (but not a magazine that would be rated "R" or "X").

## CARDS FOR TEACHING

Use playing cards with your preschoolers for teaching numbers and colors, matching suits, counting, and simple addition. Kids can line up the cards to make roads for little cars, or have fun trying to build a card house when the car is still. Even very young children enjoy playing "Slap Jacks" and "Go Fish." Children love to learn how to shuffle cards while riding, too.

## PIPE CLEANER PLAY

Pipe cleaners can be twisted into geometric shapes, people, animals, letters, numbers, necklace chains, rings, etc. When interest lags, straighten them for later use. Colored pipe cleaners used in crafts are best, not only for the colors provided, but also because they are not scratchy.

## FACE PAINTING

As suggested in the chapter "Bath Time: the Highlight of the Day," your child will enjoy painting his face as a clown, Indian, etc. This makes a super fun car activity, but be sure to use *washable* felt markers. These can be cleaned off his face with premoistened towelettes, with hand lotion, baby oil, petroleum jelly, or with plain soap and water. In the car it is especially important to give a child a nonbreakable mirror, which you can purchase at a pet supply store. They are made for parakeets.

## TAPE AS A TOY

Roll pieces of tape into circles with the sticky side out. Kids will have fun sticking them to their noses, cheeks, and each other. Baby will be fascinated with one of these circles stuck to his nose or his thumb.

Your child will also devise other ways of turning tape into a toy. He may wrap a doll as a mummy. He could make a ball from masking tape by wrapping it repeatedly around a wad of paper. He might bandage himself or another child and play doctor. Or he may use the tape to construct shapes or toys from cardboard or paper.

## SURPRISE BALLS

Before a trip of several hours, help your children make a surprise ball for each other. The idea is to have one different item for play during each thirty minutes of the trip. The child can make a ball by attaching little toys (which can also be played with) to a long crepe paper streamer. She should leave about two feet of space between the toys and wind the streamer into a ball.

At the beginning of the trip each child gives the surprise ball to the sibling for whom it was made. (Make sure each child receives one made for him.) Every half hour of the trip each child unwinds the ball until he comes to a new prize. When the last prize in each ball is found the children know the trip is nearly finished.

You do not have to purchase new toys for this. Old favorites will serve very well.


## REDUCE TRIP FATIGUE

Most traveling fatigue is caused by poor circulation. Make it a habit to stop every hour and get everyone out of the car for five minutes of exercise. Roadside rest areas are ideal, but if you cannot find any other place, a spot behind a gas station or restaurant will do.


## EXERCISE LEADERS

For each rest stop appoint a different child to be the exercise leader. He may select any active play he wishes—in which the whole family must participate (Mom and Dad too!)—and lead the activity. By alternating leaders it becomes a game and *you* don't get the brunt of, "Oh, do I *have* to exercise?" or "I'm embarrassed to do that in public."

Suggestions to make, from which leaders may select, could include throwing a beanbag or ball, having races, jumping rope, or playing tag. You might play "Follow-the-Leader," making sure to do motions which use all the muscles that have been cramped while riding. Do family calisthenics. You'll be amazed at how much more pleasant a trip you'll have by taking simple breaks. A trip without "fidgets" and "fussies" is safer and more pleasant for all. Mom and Dad will arrive at the destination much fresher, too.

## MUNCHIES

Snacks in the car can help when children are tired. Before the trip, help each child pack some of his own favorite car treats. Keep the food simple and nutritious. Remind the kids that sweets promote thirst. Fruit, raisins, unbuttered popcorn, and unsalted nuts are good choices for travel, as are fruit rolls and granola snacks. Kids also like cheese wedges and vienna sausages or cocktail weiners.

## TRYING NEW TREATS

Perhaps your children will try snacks in the car which they would not normally choose at home. Tell the kids you are making a surprise which is secret and to be used only at special times during the trip. You might pack carrot and bell pepper strips, which diminish thirst and leave the mouth refreshed.

For fun, cut small pieces of celery and pack a plastic butter spreader and a glob of peanut butter in a little plastic container. When the children need a car activity, tell them to spread peanut butter or cheese spread on the celery to make snacks for everyone in the family. For a child who doesn't think he likes raw vegetables, this is an appealing entice-ment. The veggies will stay crisp for a long time if you pack them in a zipper plastic bag with an ice cube.

## TRAVEL DRINKS

For travel drinks, let your children shop with you or choose from your preselected assortment of lunch box fruit

---

### Drinks to Avoid

Children become hyperactive and cross after consuming drinks with caffeine or artificial coloring. Avoid these when traveling. In fact, it's a good idea to avoid them, period.

juice packets or cartons (the kind that come with straws). These are easy to drink without spilling, and they eliminate the danger of glass bottles. They are also packaged in amounts a child can drink, so you don't have half-filled containers of drinks left to spill in the car.

## A WARM DRINK

On cold days, children will enjoy sipping clear soup or hot chocolate from an insulated drink container (nonbreakable, designed for school lunch boxes) that has a spout for a straw.

## THIRST QUENCHERS

For warmer weather, use a widemouthed, small insulated container that is designed to be used in a lunch box to keep soup or casseroles hot. Let your kids fill this with ice cubes to suck on when thirsty.

## GUM HELPS

When the child is thirsty, hungry, or tired from traveling, offer him a piece of sugarless gum to chew. It can help for those last few miles before you find a restaurant.

If you are unlucky enough to find that the gum has fallen out of the child's mouth and gotten stuck in his hair or on his clothing, use ice cubes to freeze the gum and work it out of the hair or clothes. Gum in the hair can be particularly stubborn. If ice fails to help, try peanut butter or cooking oil or baby oil. These will loosen the gum so it can be combed out of the hair, but a shampoo will be necessary.

## JUG ALONG

The children will also enjoy having their own water bottles in the car. Before the trip, prepare a clean, one-quart plastic milk jug for each child. Have him write his name on it with a *permanent* marker. Children who cannot yet write their names can draw pictures or simply mark with a particular color marker on their jugs.

Each child should fill his or her jug with water and place it in the freezer the night before the trip. Have the child tape a note to the car window so the frozen water jugs are not forgotten.

Kids will have fun sipping from their jugs as the water melts during the trip. They can refill these with cool water at service stations along the way. The novelty of drinking from the jug will make water seem more special than sweet drinks, which leave a bad aftertaste.

Of course, if the water is spilled in the car, it is not as much of a problem as other drinks would be. And you can pour a little water onto a handkerchief for quick face washing or onto cotton swabs for "paint-with-water books."

## SAVING MONEY

On a long trip water jugs can save quite a bit of money. If children complain about drinking water instead of buying canned drinks along the way, you might teach a good lesson about delaying gratification and saving for something more worthwhile.

Have a special family savings purse. At each gas stop along the way give the children the cost of one canned drink for each family member to place in the purse. If you can afford to spend the money, you might vote on a special family splurge on which to spend the money near the end of the trip. If you cannot afford a splurge, the children can count the money at the end of the trip to see how much would have been wasted on soft drinks. This will be a valuable lesson that your children will recall many times during their lives.

## TIME FOR LEARNING

The time with the family locked together in the car can be a wonderful communication time without the interruptions of a telephone or TV. Use the opportunity to tell your children about when you were a child, how Mom and Dad met, family history and genealogy. Encourage your children to tell you about their friends, their feelings, and their school. It's a good opportunity for teaching moral lessons, too.

You might pack a book about the "birds and bees" and have the kids take turns reading it aloud as you ride along. In the car you have a captive audience for sex education. Because you are not face-to-face, the embarrassment level for parents and children is lessened. Keep conversations open and encourage the children to ask questions.

## STUDY NATURE

When you have rest stops on a trip, collect wildflowers, dead butterflies, rocks, and leaves. Get a small nature book for your glove compartment. When the trip resumes, help the kids locate their finds in the book and identify them.

## NATURE CONTEST

Have a contest for drawing and coloring pictures of flowers, rocks, bark, leaves, insects, butterflies, animals, trees, or anything else you see or collect as you travel.

## OBSERVING AND SHARING

After a rest stop, you might ask the children to draw something they observed while out of the car, then tell each other about the picture and the experience.

## USE MAGNIFIERS

Keep a small plastic magnifier in the car where your children can easily locate it to inspect a leaf, rock, or butterfly wing more closely. Not only does this occupy the kids during the rest stops as well as during the subsequent time when riding, but it also makes learning a habit of life every day, wherever they are. Your children will associate learning with fun and family togetherness, and that will reinforce the positive aspects of the learning experience. They will not have the mistaken idea that learning is confined to the schoolroom.

## INCREASE AWARENESS

Play a game when you are in the car. Ask the children to close their eyes at a certain point in the route. Say, "We are passing Mr. Brown's house; what is on the other side of the street?" Or, "We are at the intersection of Main Street and Central Avenue; how many blocks is it to your school?" This type of activity will increase your child's (and your own) awareness of his surroundings. It will help younger siblings to learn how to figure out where they are and how to get home. It could help if they are ever lost. But just as important, children become more observant of the details of their daily lives.

## LITTLE GUIDES

When you enter a store or shopping center, tell your youngest child it is his duty to observe what you pass and direct you back to the car when you are finished shopping. This can be very helpful when you are in a large mall and have forgotten where you left the car. When inside the center, ask your older children to tell you which way is north.

## LEARNING TO OBSERVE

Have you encouraged your children to be observant and to take and give directions well? Children often watch details more carefully than adults. The next time you take a familiar route, ask your preschooler to direct you by telling you which turns to take to get home. Ask older children the names of the streets before you arrive at the turns. See if they can tell you whether the turn is right or left, north, south, east, or west. You may be pleasantly surprised. On the other hand, you may be amazed that teens who are begging to drive cannot even name the streets they commonly traverse!

## PLOTTING FUN

Give the children a map and have them plot your trip and figure out the mileage from place to place. This is excellent for learning to read map legends and symbols. If a youngster asks, "How much longer 'til we get there?" have him compute the answer himself, by reading the map and the speedometer and doing a little math. Have a contest for figuring times and distances to other places.

## SEEK AND FIND

Play "Seek and Find" by giving clues to something you see. The first child to see and identify the object becomes the one who gives the next clues.

## ALPHABET GAMES

Alphabet games have several different versions. One is to find the letters of the alphabet in order on signs you pass. To claim a letter, the child must see it on a sign on his side of the car and must be the first to claim that particular word on that sign.

Another alphabet game is good for memory training. One player says, "I'm going on a trip and taking an Apple." The next must name the same "A" word and add a "B" word. Toward the end of the alphabet, remembering all the items is quite a feat.

## DESCRIPTIONS

Have each child make a list of twenty-five words to describe himself.

## MOTION PICTURES

Bumpy drawings are always surprising. Have each child hold a felt-tipped marker lightly on a piece of paper. As the car moves along the marker will "draw a picture." The one holding the pen decides silently what the picture looks like and asks others to guess.

## JUNIOR ORNITHOLOGISTS

Give each of your children a small notebook before the trip and have a contest for seeing and listing the most birds along the way. Take a bird book for identification. The same can be done with trees and wildflowers. This is an especially good way to make children aware that wildlife varies from area to area. (See "Loving Nature Is Natural" chapter.)

## YOUR TURN

Continued stories encourage creativity. One person begins a story. At an exciting point he stops and another continues. (See Index for other story ideas.)

## USING THE NEWS

Talk about news items that you hear on the car radio. Explain concepts such as "Disarmament" to your children.

## NEWS CLIP

Clip out famous faces from a newspaper. Have a contest to see which child can name the most. In the beginning of the trip the children may not know any of the faces, but by the time you return home, they will recognize all these celebrities. (For other learning activities with newspapers, see Index.)

## NAME THE TUNE

Teenagers will have fun playing "Name the Tune" with parents. When a popular song comes on the radio, kids can ask parents to identify the singer or performer. If the teen brought along a cassette player, ask him to play just a few seconds of his favorite tape, and see if you can identify the song and the group. Ask him to tell you about the music he enjoys. You will be getting to know your child better.

## MATH FUN

Tell your child how old you were when he was born, and have him figure out how old you are now. Do this for other members of the family and for future years. For instance, "When you are 23, how old will I be?"

## SILLY LINES

Composing limericks as you ride in the car can be great family fun. Limericks are silly poems of five lines. The rhyme pattern is A,A,B,B,A. Example:

> Said Dad while driving the car,
> "We really shouldn't go this far."
> But he turned to the right,
> And he drove all night,
> And we ended up on a star!

Children will get into the composing mood quickly and laugh at the silly rhymes that result. This is especially funny when you allow each person to make up only one line.

## DRAWING AND GUESSING

Give the children the car magnifier (a nonbreakable one), and ask them to draw an enlarged portion of some natural find, perhaps a segment of a butterfly wing, as they see it through the magnifier. Comment that if they draw an enlarged segment, as seen through the magnifier, instead of the whole object, pictures become abstract in appearance and difficult to identify. This lends itself to a guessing game for other people in the car to guess from the picture what object has been observed under the magnifier.

## READ ALOUD

Keep in the car a good read-aloud book, which the family can enjoy together. Children can practice diction and expression skills. Tell them to let their eyes run ahead of their voice when reading aloud. You may finish the book on one trip, or you may read it on errands around town for months.

## LOG IT IN

Travelogues will become souvenirs that make the trip memorable. Purchase an artist's sketch pad with a spiral binding and good quality paper for each child. The pages are stronger and will last years longer than typical "scrapbook" pages. As the child collects travel folders, maps, ticket stubs and postcards, have him develop his scrapbook. Items can be taped, stapled, or glued onto the pages as you travel from one place to another.

## ARTISTIC MEMOIRS

Take a package of typing paper and have each child draw his favorite place visited during each day. Ask him to describe the day's event in a few sentences below the drawing. He can place these in a loose-leaf notebook about the trip. When you return home he can add pages of photos taken along the way.

## HEAR, HEAR!

Cassette players are wonderful on a trip. Give each child his own blank tape. Children will adore recording their own voices singing or telling a story, making up a play, interviewing family members about given subjects, or just creating sound effects.

## RECORD MEMORIES

At the end of every day of the trip bring out a special blank tape. Record each member of the family talking about the events of the day. Your family will enjoy these memories for years to come, especially after little voices have grown more mature.

## SURPRISE TAPE

If you think your children might become self-conscious or reluctant to record their impressions of the trip, you might turn on the recorder at some point during each day's travel when no one suspects and direct the family conversation to, "Wasn't it fun when . . . ?" or "What did you like best about . . . ?" Keep the tape a secret and surprise the family when you return home. Everyone will be delighted to hear the tape, even if someone is a little embarrassed to hear his own voice.

## NIGHT ACTIVITIES

Take a star chart, a tiny flashlight, and some binoculars (if you have them) for your children to learn about the night-time sky as you ride. When you are traversing a lonely stretch of road on a clear night, there are numerous stars visible that your children cannot see at home, unless you live far from city lights. In order to study the star charts without altering your vision for referring to the sky, cover the tiny flashlight beam with a piece of red cellophane held on with a rubber band. It is safer to reserve binocular use for rest stops.

## HEAVENLY SEARCH

Many games for car play require no equipment but can stimulate the imagination and while away the hours on a long trip. Encourage children to entertain themselves silently by finding pictures in clouds.

This can also become a family guessing game called "Do You See What I See?" One child discovers a cloud which seems to form a picture and indicates which cloud the others should study in order to guess what he sees.

## ENCOURAGING SLEEP

Studying the sky for cloud pictures or constellations is a good activity if you want your children to fall asleep. Tell them they can see the skies best if they lie down (keeping seat belts fastened). They will likely fall asleep doing this quiet activity, day or night. Be sure to do this just *after* a gas or bathroom stop.

## TRIPS BY AIR

If the travel bug really bites you, sooner or later you will most likely travel by air with your children. Although many of the ideas for car travel can be used when traveling by air, here are some ideas especially designed to help make flights a fun adventure for your entire family. The children will be excited about flying, and with a little preplanning you, too, can enjoy the trip and use it to teach your children as well as delight them.

Of course, breast-fed babies are the most "portable," because there is no worry about their food. But it can be embarrassing to nurse in public. I don't recommend the first solution I tried: I took my hungry baby to the airplane bathroom, locked the door, and began to feed him. After about 20 minutes a stewardess knocked on the door and announced very loudly, "It has been brought to our attention that you have been locked in the rest room an abnormal amount of time. Unlock this door immediately, or I shall call the captain." It never had occurred to me that they might think I was planting a bomb!

## Keep Ears Clear

Have your baby suck a pacifier or bottle, or nurse at the breast during takeoff and landing when air pressure is changing. It will ease his discomfort and prevent screaming. If your child has an ear infection or stuffy nose, ask your doctor about a prescription for an antihistamine, to be given about 30 minutes prior to takeoff, to keep nasal and ear passages clear. This is very important.

If you are planning your first flight with children, it is nice to know that disposable diapers are usually available during the flight and that the stewardess will be happy to refrigerate or warm the baby's bottle or food, if necessary. Babies are usually no problem in flight.

When making plane reservations, order children's meals for the other children in your family. During the flight ask for a "Kids' Kit" for entertainment of young children. Some airlines will give older children a deck of playing cards, on request.

### PITCH A TENT

Baby will be very contented nursing from Mom's breast in an airport or plane. For the sake of modesty, make a nursing "tent." In the center of a 45-inch square of material, cut a slit for Mom's head. Bind this slit with bias tape. You can make the tent beautiful with embroidery, lace, ribbon, etc. (This makes a great baby shower gift!) Or you can keep it quick and simple by cutting the edges with pinking shears, eliminating even the need for hems. When baby wants to be fed, simply pull the tent over your head, and baby will be cozy beneath it, nursing in peaceful bliss.

### TURTLE BACK RIDES

Help each of your children prepare a backpack for travel entertainment. (Look at suggestions for contents of a Happy Kit, earlier in this chapter.) It helps to have the children pack these backpacks about a week before they travel, so the toys will be novel and interesting again during the trip. Help your children select small, lightweight toys, and limit the number so the packs remain light and not bulging.

Just before the trip add the child's security blanket or stuffed animal. Also be sure to have a jacket, because planes are often cold. I always put each child's running suit in for all-over warmth and comfort, and for a change of clothes just in case our suitcases do not arrive when we do.

## HAPPY, HAPPY HOUR

Although airlines provide meals, they are notoriously late. Many a midair "happy hour" has turned into a very "unhappy hour" for parents of young travelers. Pack nutritious snacks in a hidden bag of treats so that a delayed meal will not ruin the fun of the plane trip. When your children are hungry pull out some tasty treats such as peanut butter crackers, raisins, an apple, or granola snack bars.

## JOLLY JUMPERS

Plane travel can be tiring. Encourage the children to go to the rest room to do a few jumping jacks during the flight. You might initiate some in-seat exercises also. Isometrics are fun for children and don't disturb other travelers. Tell the kids to place their hands with palms together and press as hard as they can, until their muscles tremble. Then have them lock fingers and try to pull their hands apart.

An isometric exercise for cramped little legs is to cross the ankles and attempt to pull the feet apart with ankles "locked" together. They can alternate this with pushing the knees together as tightly as possible. Tell the children to have contests with each other to see who can do each isometric exercise the longest. You might time them with your watch. (One with a stopwatch feature is especially helpful.)

## OPEN WIDE

During takeoff and landing, offer the kids their favorite chewing gum (sugarless is recommended by dentists). Have the children compete to see which one can open his mouth the widest when chewing. This equalizes air pressure on the eardrum and alleviates ear discomfort.

## YAWNING CONTESTS

If a child complains about his ears during the flight, you might try yawning contests. Show the child how to force a yawn by thinking about yawning and slowly stretching his lower jaw forward and downward. It can become a game to see who can make the other one yawn, since yawning seems to come on by the power of suggestion.

## AIR PRESSURE LESSONS

Before the trip, ask your doctor, local health department, or school for a photocopy picture of the middle ear and Eustachian tube. When older children feel ear discomfort during a flight, it is an opportune time to teach them about air pressure and their own ears. Explain that at sea level atmospheric pressure on the body is 14.69 pounds per square inch. Children will be fascinated with the concept that air has weight and that as they rise into the air that weight or pressure becomes less.

Show the physiology pictures and explain that the eardrum is like the covering on a drum, which can be pushed inward or outward with pressure. Point out the Eustachian tube and tell the kids that one of its functions is to allow air from the throat to equalize pressure behind the eardrum with the air pressure from the outer ear. The discomfort of the eardrum as the plane gains altitude results because the membrane is pushing outward since the pressure is not equalized. Yawning or opening the mouth wide allows the air pressure to become equalized on both sides of the eardrum.

## ENJOY THE ADVENTURE

It is important for Moms and Dads to get away with just each other sometimes. But it is also important to give your children the opportunity to travel when you can afford it. With the ideas in this chapter, I hope you have seen that traveling is an adventure and a learning experience that can be enjoyed by all members of the family together, whether it is just a ride in the country on Sunday afternoon, or a flight to exotic places. Children who experience other people and places grow up more adaptable, with self-confidence in new situations and more tolerance toward all people. Don't wait until your children are grown to enjoy new adventures.

# DOLLARS AND SENSE

I t is difficult to find the fine line of balance between teaching your children about money and teaching them to be materialistic. A child needs to learn about money in order to be able to use it wisely. From the time he first learns to talk, he begins to beg for items he has seen advertised on TV. Television teaches us constantly to want more and more, and advertisers know children are their most vulnerable victims. No mother can take a child through a grocery store without the whine of, "Get this cereal. They say on TV it's the best," or "This one has my favorite prize in it." At the checkout counter merchants have conveniently placed the most appealing items at a little one's eye level.

When my newspaper feature, *Formulas For Fun,* first began to appear in our local paper, I became paranoid that everyone was watching my children and looking for model behavior in them because I was writing a parental advice column. Several weeks later, our four-year-old, Tommy, oblivious to the fact that his behavior was now open to public scrutiny, let the world know he was no one's model child. He and I were waiting in line at the checkout counter of the grocery store, when he decided he *had* to have a candy bar.

After being told several times that he could not have it because it was lunchtime, he began to cry.

Now, one of my readers had written to me that a good way to discipline a child in a public place when a spanking was definitely *not* in order, was to pinch him, getting prompt attention and resulting in model behavior. Since my policy was never to recommend anything I had not personally tested, I thought this was a good time to try this terrific idea.

I said quietly but sternly, "Tommy, you may not have the candy. Now straighten up and behave," and I firmly pinched his arm. Tommy looked at my face, then at the candy bar, then at the long line of unconcerned shoppers and screamed, "Child Abuse! My mother did child abuse to me!" And he threw himself on the floor crying hysterically. I wanted to vanish right then and there in front of the newsstand bearing my photograph and my column about good parenting.

It would be easier and less embarrassing to succumb to the tearful pleas of youngsters in order to get out of the store without a further scene. But what would this teach our children?

1. That they can get anything they want by crying.

2. That they must not be satisfied merely with what they have, but constantly want more.

3. That every time parents go to a store the child gets to buy something.

4. That pleasure is derived by spending money.

Do we really want our children to file away these statements in their subconscious minds to be used as references through life? Because a child begins at a very early age to want to purchase items, we must begin to teach him at a very early age to handle money thoughtfully and wisely.

To teach your child to be money wise there are a few "Never, Nevers" that will help you. One is: while you are doing necessary shopping, never be talked into buying the child a whim item just because he whines for it. If the child once is allowed to do this, he will continue the whining and begging on every shopping trip.

Never take a child "wish shopping." This promotes materialism and unnecessary spending and develops very dangerous habits which could last throughout his life. It promotes the idea of being dissatisfied with what you have and always wanting more. It creates the idea that spending money promotes happiness.

If a child wants to purchase something with his own money, he should have in mind what he intends to purchase *before* going to the store. He may sometimes change his mind after looking at the item, but he should not be allowed to go into a store with a pocketful of money and just look for a way to spend it.

Another thing that parents should avoid is allowing the child to purchase an item before he has earned the money for it. This develops the habit of spending beyond his means and is one of the major reasons why adults get overextended on charge accounts. Do not allow the child to learn this dangerous habit. Also, after the item is purchased the incentive to work for it is gone. You will have a terrible time getting him to do the jobs to pay for that item because he already has it, and there will always be another one he wants.

Gambling is a very dangerous trap into which many children fall at an early age. It begins with youngsters betting on a football game, on pinball machines, or on video games. These quarters gambled seem harmless. By teen years the gambling amounts have increased to five-, ten-, or twenty-dollar wagers placed on golf matches, etc.

From whom do children learn most bad habits, which could become all-encompassing and destroy their future security? Set a good example for your children in all your money management. This chapter will give you ideas on how you can teach your children to become, perhaps, even better able than you to manage their dollars with sense.

## HELPING LITTLE CHILDREN LEARN ABOUT MONEY

The first step with preschoolers is to teach them to identify various coins, and to learn how to get money and how to use it. Teaching the wisest use of money from the very first will develop good habits in your child so that he continues them throughout life, almost without thinking, and becomes a good money manager. Read on for some fun ways to help your preschoolers learn.

## YOUNGSTERS AT PLAY

Let the child make coin rubbings for entertainment, in order to familiarize her with different sizes and imprints. Place a coin under a sheet of paper. Bearing down firmly with a "fat" pencil or crayon, the child can rub over the coin until its imprint is clearly revealed.

It is also fun to do this without marking on the paper, rubbing it instead with a firm object, perhaps the cap to a ballpoint pen. By doing the rubbing this way, the child will see only the embossed image without any color. Crisp paper must be used for this second method, or aluminum foil. If foil is used, the child may want to cut out the embossed circles and use them for play money.

## TEST HER MEMORY

Just for fun have your child use a compass to draw circles of five different sizes on plain paper and cut them out. Now ask her to pretend they are coins and to draw from memory what is on each coin. Have her practice this at various times until she can draw the fronts and backs of each coin.

Now she can have the fun of asking other adults to try the test. Although we handle coins every day, few adults will be able to tell her exactly what is on the face and back of every coin. Children are more detail-conscious than most adults because they learn by observation. We seldom notice the details of those things most familiar to us. By doing this little test and game you are not only teaching your child about coins but also to be observant and to remember what she sees. This will carry over into other areas.

## COIN CHART

Ask your youngster to make a money chart for her room. She can draw and color each coin in a very enlarged size. Mount these on poster paper and help her write the value beside each coin. Be sure to include the "cents" sign beside each and explain to the child what it means. Beside each drawing glue on an actual coin. Post the chart in a place where she will see it often.

## LEARNING TO COUNT

Teach counting by using coins. Give the child 100 pennies to keep in a plastic container (when he is old enough to be trusted not to put them in his mouth). Using a second container, have him practice each day counting as many pennies as he can, placing them into the second container until he makes a mistake. The next day, have him first count the ones he counted correctly the previous day, to be sure he can still do it without error. See how many pennies he can add each day. Tell him that when he can count 100 pennies without error for five days in a row, you will take him to the store to buy something with them. Be sure to name an item (perhaps doughnuts or gumballs from a machine or balloons) which he can purchase for 100 pennies, so that he doesn't demand a bicycle when you arrive at the store! At this stage he does not yet have the concept of the value of the coins.

When he has mastered counting to 100 with pennies, next give him dimes and have him learn to count to 100 by tens in the same manner. Then repeat the exercise with nickels to teach counting by fives. Reward the child by allowing him to spend the coins when he has mastered the counting.

## DOLLAR CHART

By kindergarten age, the child is well aware of how much the toys he wants cost and that it takes lots of jobs to earn them. Help him make a chart for his room, showing the different denominations of folding money and also the dollar coin. You will not want to attach the larger, real bills to his chart, but you may wish to glue on a dollar coin and staple on a real one-dollar bill. Let him draw the others on green construction paper and cut them out for his chart.

Have the child draw the different bills to the best of his ability, front and back. This will help him to observe and remember the way they look. It will also be an introduction to the presidents of the United States and other important people depicted on our money. Observe the designs with him and talk with him about who the people are and what the buildings are and what the inscriptions mean. You can look up the information for the larger bills in the encyclopedia. Or take the child to your bank and request that he see the larger bills in order to know what they look like. You might cash a check for a large bill, show it to your child, then redeposit it.

## GIVING KIDS MONEY

When your child learns that money buys things he wants, he will want more and more of it. Fixed allowances are a commonly used method for giving the child spending money. The advantage of an allowance is that the child knows how much money he will have and can learn to budget and save for things he wants. Allowance amounts vary with the age of the child and the income of the parents. Many parents have set chores for the child to do weekly to earn the allowance, but often parents fall into the trap of giving the allowance even if the jobs have not been done.

Some parents are firmly opposed to allowances. They believe that a child should learn from the beginning that money is *earned*. That is the way the world works, so he might as well learn this from the start. Read on for ways of solving this dilemma in your home.

### WORK FOR MONEY

There are many jobs even a two-year-old can do: picking up his toys, carrying his dishes to the sink, bringing in the newspaper, feeding the dog, picking up items you drop, drying nonbreakable dishes. Whatever the child's age, he will find satisfaction in doing a job well and receiving *praise* and, sometimes, a reward in the form of a special privilege, his favorite food, or an outing.

If you prefer to give your children monetary remuneration for jobs done, find several jobs each child can do for you and set the value of the job according to his age and the difficulty of the task. For instance, a very young child does not need much money, so you might pay him a few pennies for each simple job he does.

When he completes his job, take time to inspect his work and praise him or show him how he can improve. Help him make the improvement and encourage his sense of personal satisfaction in a job well done. Then give him his financial reward.

It is very important that you pay him at the time he performs the job. A young child will not understand that the pay is for the job if you do not pay him at the time he performs it. Keep a jar of pennies hidden so that you have them when you need them. Or keep a few in your pocket each day so they are handy and you don't have to stop to search for them.

## CAREFUL WITH COINS

If the child is still young enough to put things into his mouth, get a bank which he cannot open. Help him place the penny immediately into his bank. He can shake it and periodically open it with you in order to count his money. Perhaps he can buy a package of gum, with his own money, when you go to the grocery store each week. You could make sure he earns enough money for that package of gum weekly.

## THREE BANKS

Purchase not one but three banks for your child: one for savings, one for petty cash or spending money, and one for giving. Be sure the three banks look very different from each other so the child will not accidentally confuse them. With a permanent marker write on each bank its purpose.

When you begin to pay a little one for his simple jobs, perhaps you can give him three pennies for each job instead of just one. He will begin the habit of putting one penny into each bank from the first. As he grows and can understand the concepts of spending, saving, and giving he will later understand portions or percentages. Then you can further develop the habits with more thought as to choices and percentages. But with little ones, a penny per bank per job is an easy way to begin.

## LEARNING TO SAVE

Have the child lift the savings and spending banks (see above) each week to see which is heavier. He will notice that the savings bank grows heavier each week while the spending bank does not. Tell him that when he spends money it is gone. When he saves it he still has it, the amount grows each week, and he can buy something better than if he had spent the money right away.

## LEARNING GENEROSITY

Watch for charitable opportunities with kid appeal. Encourage your child to empty his "Giving Bank" and give the pennies he has earned. Show him news and TV pictures of hungry children, and take him with you if you help with programs like "Meals on Wheels" for the elderly or projects which help families who have lost their homes. Help the child be aware of others less fortunate than he and look for opportunities to help with his own money.

One second grader I know noticed that a poor boy in his class walked to school every day and had frequent colds and earaches. Since the boy had no hat, the second grader used his "giving money" to purchase a stocking cap to keep the boy warm. You cannot begin too early to teach your children to be compassionate and generous.

The generous child will feel happy knowing that *he himself* has earned the money to give. Teach him that when he gives he should always give part of himself. Have him contrast the feeling he has after giving his own money to a charity (with which he empathizes) to the feeling he gets if you just hand him some money to put in the Salvation Army bell-ringer's or the March of Dimes can. Talk to him about the good feeling he gets when he gives money he has earned. Tell him that feeling of true compassion and generosity is not the same if he is giving money someone else has earned.

## EARNING MORE MONEY

As your child grows you will want to make the jobs a little larger and the pay a little more, but keep both job and payment appropriate for his age. Sometimes the incentive is lacking for jobs the child does not like. Perhaps you can use a different incentive. For instance, if your child is required to pull some weeds and he is grumbling about it, ask, "If you saw a whole field of pennies, would you stop to pick them up?" Of course, he would! Answer, "Well, pretend each weed is a penny you are picking up, and I'll pay you a penny for each one that you pull up with a root on it." The same idea works well for picking up branches or twigs after a storm.

## "A PENNY SAVED . . ."

There are other jobs which pay more than the amount of work involved is actually worth, but these jobs teach valuable lessons about saving money. For instance, when you are paying bills tell your child that it costs quite a lot of money to buy stamps. Tell him if he will deliver your bill payment for you, you will give him the price of the stamp he is saving you. Select about six payments which go to an area close to each other and go with the child to these places.

Go with your child to pay a few bills in person. Have the child go alone to the payment window and greet the person, hand her the envelope, and wait for the receipt. Besides teaching the "penny saved, penny earned" concept, it shows your child the necessity of paying bills regularly and that things like electricity and water are not free. But, best of all, it helps your youngster learn to meet people, speak on his own, take responsibility, and develop self-confidence. It is an excellent teaching experience and a wonderful way for your child to earn a good bit of money in a fairly painless way.

You might go to a gas station and pay your child the difference between the self-service and full-service price of gas, if he will fill the tank for you.

## CHEER UP!

For more fun with coins you can save the change from your pockets each day and collect it in a coffee can. When a youngster has had a disappointing day or is sick, give him the can of coins and some rollers and tell him he can keep all the rolls of coins he can make correctly. It will occupy him for hours and make him feel special. The easiest way to start a coin roll is to push the first few coins in with a pencil. You may have to start the rolls for the child. Have him carefully count out the coins which should fit into each roll. The sorting of the change into piles of dollars is good experience as well as fun.

## THE COLLECTOR

Another way to sort the coins, if he is not interested in rolling them, is by years. Have the child notice differences in some coins of the same denomination, and explain that, periodically, coins are redesigned. Talk about coins becoming more valuable as they become rare. Get a beginner's book on coin collecting and visit coin shops with your child. It can become a lifelong hobby.

## OLDER CHILDREN LEARN HOW MONEY WORKS

By school age, children who have done the things suggested earlier in this chapter will be ready to learn about different coin equivalents. It is a good way to begin some math concepts. The old coin charts in their rooms have now been learned by heart. Give the child a portion of his closet to clean really well and then reward him by removing all the money from the coin charts and allowing him to keep it.

### TEACHING COIN EQUIVALENTS

Help your elementary-age children make coin equivalent charts for their rooms. These are different from the charts in the earlier part of this chapter. Have your child attach a nickel, make a prominent "equals" sign and attach five pennies, with the words "one nickel equals five pennies." Tell the child who cannot at first understand the concept that it means five pennies can hide inside the nickel. Ask the child how much a nickel is worth. Have him hold out his hand with five fingers outstretched, palm up. Place five pennies in it. Lay several coins, including one nickel, on a table and ask him to choose the one that equals those five pennies in his hand.

When he selects the nickel have him hold it in his other hand. Now play storekeeper and hold an item worth a nickel, perhaps a sucker. Tell him to purchase it from you. Tell him the cost is "five cents." He can choose which way to pay you, with the nickel or the pennies. "Which hand do you want to use to pay for the sucker? Each one holds the same amount of money."

When you feel the child thoroughly understands this, add a second line to your new chart. This line should read, "a dime equals two nickels equals ten pennies." Again play storekeeper, using the various ways to pay the ten cents until the child understands that each way is the same amount of money.

Continue your chart and game with a quarter, a fifty-cent piece, and a dollar. This, of course, will not be done all in one day. It may take quite awhile for the youngster to grasp the concepts.

## PLAY STORE

After the equals chart (see above) is fairly well mastered, tell the child you are playing grocery store. He is to buy three apples from you. Each apple costs twenty-five cents, but you want him to pay you in a different way for each apple. Give him a handful of coins and let him make the choices, purchasing each apple separately from you and each time giving you a different combination of coins to make the twenty-five cents.

## CASH REGISTER

Youngsters always enjoy playing with a toy cash register. Play the storekeeper game, with your child paying you in bills and making change. Then have him be the storekeeper and make change for you. This takes endless practice and lots of thinking for little minds, but can be a game of endless fun, too. Teach him always to recount his change when he receives it from a clerk. Anyone can make a mistake.

Many hours of learning can occur while playing store. Give kids cans from your pantry to play with and either real or play money to make their purchases.

## PLAY MONEY

Children can make their own play money by drawing the coins and bills on construction paper. Have them draw each different denomination of coins and bills on one sheet of paper. Then let the children photocopy it. They can cut out the coins and have as many different pieces of play money as they wish.

Teach your children that they must not photocopy real paper money. This is an excellent time to introduce the concept of what money really is: a promise from the government that the official bill or coin has purchasing power and is acceptable as a trade medium. Teach your children that the paper money they make is not official, not made by the government, so it cannot be spent.

If you have the opportunity to visit a mint with your child, do so.

## MONEY GAMES

By the time your children are in upper-elementary grades they will enjoy playing family games that use money, such as Monopoly, Stocks and Bonds, Masterpiece, and The Game of Life, for more practice in money concepts and making change.

## PERCENTAGES

By school age, when the child thoroughly understands about the different values of coins, it is time to talk about how he will apportion his money among the three banks. (See above.) A good balance is to teach him to place one dime out of every dollar in his "Giving Bank," and four dimes out of every dollar into his "Savings Bank." At this stage I recommend getting a fourth bank. The "Spending Bank" should be divided into two parts. The child by now has had enough experience with money to understand that sometimes he spends his money on something he can enjoy for a long time, perhaps a toy. There are other things he buys which are like throwing the money away because the item is gone almost immediately, for example soft drinks, candy, video machines, and movies.

If you have two different spending banks you can help the child to learn to limit the money he spends on things that are quickly gone. Perhaps he will put one dime into the spending bank marked "Throwaway Money." The other four dimes can go into the "Spending To Keep" bank, to be used for items which will last for more than a day.

## SPENDING MONEY ON OUTINGS

When going on trips or to amusement parks your child will always find hundreds of souvenir items he wants to buy. Help him earn money for the outing before going. Find a safe means for him to carry his own money. My children decided a shoe purse is the safest and easiest way to keep their money. It has a Velcro closure, attaches to shoelaces, is clearly visible, and is virtually impossible to pickpocket. Make sure you and the child know how much money he has before the outing and that he understands that when the money is gone, there is no more to spend.

Talk to him to set guidelines of whether or not he has to purchase his own food, drinks, etc. When souvenir shopping, remind him that he can look all day and come back later to make the purchase when he is really sure the item is exactly what he wants.

Help him inspect carefully the item he chooses. Tell him to consider these things: Will it break quickly? Are there any potentially harmful features? Will he still like it when he is back home? Is it worth the price? Could he purchase the same item for less money if it were not at a souvenir stand? There will always be more attractive items after the money is spent; but do not give in and allow him to buy something else after he has used up all his money. This will be a valuable lesson in money for life.

## SELECTING CHORES

Just as you have favorite jobs and jobs you detest, your child does, too. Talk to him about these feelings. Tell him that to be happy in life people should try to be in jobs they like, and that this is why it is important to be well-trained and educated for the kind of job he will enjoy.

It is important to recognize that there are many different

types of jobs which can render the same pay. Give your child a list of different jobs he can do around the house and the monetary value of each. Be sure to list at least three different kinds of jobs for the same pay. Let your child choose a certain number of these to do each day or week. A good rule is to choose five jobs he likes and one he dislikes to do each day. Explain that in life we often have to perform tasks we dislike which, nevertheless, have to be done; but we want to spend most of our time doing jobs we prefer.

## TEACHING THOUGHTFULNESS

Tell your child there are jobs that should be done over and above his chores for pay. These are jobs that are done for duty or for love, without pay. For instance, he should keep his room neat and his toys picked up, just because it is his home and he is considerate of others around him and takes pride in his own room.

There are times he should take the opportunity to do extra jobs to show thoughtfulness and love. For example, if Mother is sick or company is coming he can set the table and prepare a simple meal or wash the dishes, just to show his concern and caring. Perhaps Dad has taken time to play tennis with the youngster or to teach the teenager how to change the oil in his car. Teach the kids to be thoughtful and say "Thank you," by looking for an extra job to do for Dad in return.

## EMPLOYMENT

Sometimes a child wants something that the family cannot afford and she will have to earn the money for it outside the home. This is not impossible for even elementary-age children to do. Talk to your child about her capabilities and interests which could become profitable income sources for her. Perhaps she could baby-sit a younger neighbor at your house (where you are also nearby to watch), care for a friend's pet or houseplants while the friend is out of town, wash cars, sweep driveways or porches, or groom pets.

Of course, most children have tried selling lemonade, but if your youngster seriously needs to earn more than a little money, take him to a good location for the lemonade sale, perhaps a baseball practice field or a public park. Check your city's regulations. You may need a license to do so.

# TEENS BECOME WISE MONEY HANDLERS

If you have followed the suggestions in this chapter through the years, your teenager has an excellent understanding of money—how to earn it and how to use it wisely.

The savings bank should have been used regularly to purchase items of higher value than he could earn quickly. This delayed gratification is an important thing to learn in developing money concepts. Now it should be extended. The child is past the small toy stage; now, all his toys are more expensive but are mostly items that he will enjoy into adulthood.

## SHOPPING WISELY

Teach your teen to shop wisely. Show him various reports for consumers and help him research the quality of items before expenditures are made. Read with him all instructions. Help him mail in warranties immediately, and take him to the store or manufacturer to return inferior items. Talk to him about being a wise consumer. Encourage him to care properly for the items he has worked to purchase. Take time to appreciate and learn about each of the purchases your child makes. Share with him his enthusiasm and his pride over what he has earned and selected. Congratulate him whenever he demonstrates good habits with money.

## MAKING MONEY GO FURTHER

Teach the child that his money will go further if he makes it a habit to purchase at discount stores and to wait for sales. Show him how to watch the newspapers for sales. After Christmas take him to purchase a toy or sports equipment at half price. Teach him about seasonal sales and regular promotions. Give him money to purchase clothes and help him watch for half-price, end-of-season sales, if he has finished growing. Point out that these sales are usually held while the apparel is still "in-season", since stores stock far ahead for the next season.

Help your teen make a scrapbook of sales on large items for a year. He can clip sales ads each month. The following year he can compare the scrapbook to current ads each month. He may enjoy making his own projection chart to show which items will be on sale in which months of the year and the approximate percentage of reductions. Statistics such as these are available from various consumer organizations or from the stores, themselves.

Your teen may not want to do his own research in this manner, but if he learns about delayed gratification, it will make waiting for a sale more bearable all through life. Point out to him that if this becomes a habit he will save himself literally thousands of dollars during his lifetime and be able to make his money go nearly twice as far.

## DELAY PURCHASES

Another good practice to teach your youngster is never to buy something without first leaving the store to reconsider the purchase. The item will almost always be there tomorrow, and sometimes at a cheaper price. High-pressure salesmen, attractive advertising, and promotional merchandising have been the secrets of making people buy now and wish later they had not.

## STAY AWAY

Teach your child that the best way to save money is not to go to stores. Teens have a habit of hanging out at the local record shop or fast-food place and seem to leave with empty pockets, no matter how good their intentions.

## SLIPPERY MONEY

If your teen seems to let money slip through his fingers, give him a little pocket calendar and have him jot down expenditures each day and also what he purchases with the money. At the end of two weeks, have him add up the amount spent on food, entertainment, etc. He will learn far more from this self-taught lesson than if you just tell him he is wasting money.

Of course, when he suddenly realizes he wasted ten dollars last month on snack food at the local hangout, your grocery bill may suddenly go up because he may bring his friends home for free snacks! If this becomes a problem, you could suggest that the kids form an after-school hang-out club and go to a different home each day of the week for "free" food. Or have each child purchase one package of favorite snack items (cookies, cheese, chips, drinks, or whatever.) Then whoever makes the purchase is in charge of the rationing. Point out that making weekly bulk purchases of soft drinks, for example, is much cheaper than buying fountain drinks daily by the cup.

## TRADING

Your child should also learn that trading still exists and can be a means of getting what he wants without money or with long periods of saving. Tell your youth that what one person outgrows or tires of may be another person's dream. Have your youngster watch the want ads; go to garage sales; call the local radio station to see if they have free advertisements for swap items; talk to friends who are a little older and see if they would like to sell or trade the item they have outgrown; talk to younger friends to sell or trade their own outgrown playthings.

## SAVINGS GOALS

Talk with your child about short-term savings goals and long-term savings goals. He has learned about short-term savings by buying something he could not afford with one week's earnings but could purchase if he saved for two, perhaps. Now he needs to set aside some of his savings for long-term goals, such as an unexpected opportunity that may be his if he has the money for it. Perhaps a friend's family will invite him to go to the beach with them if he can pay his own way.

Help your youngster to plan his money management and set his goals realistically. This gives you both a mutual feeling of genuine interest and loving concern if you do it in a friendly way. Guide the youngster by asking questions that direct his thoughts, thereby helping him to make good choices for himself.

## BEHAVIOR GOALS

Special rewards should be considered to help teens stay "straight" or achieve desired behavior goals. For example, you might be able to promise your teen a special trip, a car, a computer, or something he wants more than anything else in the world if he graduates from school without using alcohol, tobacco, or drugs. Of course, the child could cheat, but his conscience would probably not allow him to. The promise from parents that they will grant him the best wish they can afford provides a marvelous crutch when the going gets tough for a teen faced with tremendous peer pressure. When your child becomes older it is easier for him to make wise decisions without being pressured by his peers if he has learned, during the tough teen years, that good behavior is its own reward and the feeling of pride is better than a feeling of shame. If you promise your child a specific reward for a specific reason, offer it as a challenge and emphasize the value of setting goals to work toward in life. Make it clear that the proposition is not a bribe.

## REWARD FOR GRADES

For the youngster who is not achieving his potential in school grades, perhaps the incentive of a certain amount of money for each letter grade he improves on the next report card will produce the desired results. But emphasize these as rewards, not bribes. There is a fine line between a bribe and a reward, and you may have difficulty devising ways to prevent the reward from becoming a bribe. One idea for rewarding good grades is to have a surprise reward, which changes each reporting period so that the child does not know what it will be. Sometimes it may be money, sometimes a special privilege or outing, sometimes the child might get to plan his favorite menu, sometimes you might post his picture on the family bulletin board for a week. This helps prevent the build-up of expectation so that the reward does not become a payment or bribe for good behavior or grades. Children should never have to be bribed to be good.

## CREATING INCOME

Before age sixteen, when a youth can legally be employed, he is capable of many money-earning jobs. Help him learn that not all jobs are types of "employment." Many jobs are created. Suggest that the youngster turn his hobby into a moneymaking project. Discuss his hobbies with the idea of making money. Perhaps he likes to draw. He could design stationery and have it printed and sell it door-to-door or on consignment in stores. He could set up a drawing board in a park and draw caricatures for pay.

Does he play tennis or golf well? He could teach lessons. Does she excel in arranging flowers? She could make and sell dried or silk arrangements. Is she good with children? Have a weekly "Play Day" for neighborhood children and charge, perhaps, five dollars for two hours of entertainment. If ten youngsters come, your teen has earned fifty dollars in two hours. It could be repeated on a weekly or biweekly basis.

Perhaps you know an invalid or elderly person who would be happy to hire some young person to run errands, prepare simple meals, shop, or even read aloud. Encourage the youth to do this sometimes just for concern, but let him know that it is also a job worthy of pay. Your child will develop a great sense of self-worth and enjoy his time much more if he is productive.

## LEARNING ABOUT BANKING

By the time he is in middle school or junior high your youngster should open a savings account at a banking institution and should regularly make deposits to it from his own savings bank. Show him about interest earned and help him calculate how much his money will increase if saved at a bank instead of at home. Assure him that the money is still his and is available to him when he wants it, but that the longer he leaves it in the bank account, the more interest it will earn.

### CHECKING ACCOUNTS

By the time a youngster can get a driver's license it is a necessity to have a checking account. There are many er-

> If your child goes by a second name or nickname, it can present a problem in identification when he wants to write a check. Be sure that the signature on his driver's license and the signature on his checks are the same.

rands the young driver can run for you, and if he can write a check it will save you a lot of trouble. Go with him to several banks to compare what is offered to youngsters. Some banks give free checks, some have lower average daily balance requirements, some have interest-earning accounts. Help your child decide which offers him the best value and meets his needs.

## BALANCE ACCOUNTS

Help your youngster learn to balance his checking account and do it each month. Give him a special place to keep together all his banking and accounting records and help him organize a system that is orderly. Show him how to post a ledger of his checks so that he knows how he spends his money. Tell him to keep all statements and canceled checks for records. If he has a computer encourage him to use it to keep his monthly records. You might hire him to keep the family accounting records.

## SAVING FOR EDUCATION

Your teen should be encouraged to save for his future education now. Talk with your youngster about his ideas about future education goals. Encourage him to get brochures from higher education facilities by writing to the institutions or by asking his own school counselor. Go over the financial expenses of these institutions with your teen. Tell him how you are planning financially for his future and what you expect to be able to afford. Encourage him to set realistic educational goals for himself and help work toward them by earning good grades or excelling in a sport or talent for the possibility of a scholarship and by saving a certain portion of his earnings for that time in the future. The youngster who helps earn his education will value it more.

## BUDGETING

Now that your youth is writing checks and posting a ledger, it is time for him to have a budget and a special allowance for clothing and personal items. Help him list all his basic needs and figure the cost of each. Explain that you have been providing these items for him but that with a checking account and a driver's license he can make the purchases and keep up with them for himself. Often what a child earns is not enough to buy all his or her own personal items. You may have to supplement his income to cover the necessities and, perhaps, have him cover the costs on the luxuries. Establish clearly with him which items you expect him to purchase with his own money and which you will pay for by placing money into his account. Decide on how much money you can give him for purchases of clothing and other items you have always bought for him, based on past costs. Your teen cannot learn to budget unless he knows clearly what he is expected to buy and unless he realistically has enough money or earning power to do so.

This will teach him the cost of living and will save you much time in shopping. It is wise to begin this the junior year in high school so that you have two years to oversee and guide him in getting accustomed to this big job before he goes out on his own. It will develop his feeling of maturity and will prepare him well for life's responsibilities.

## TAKE TIME

Each day take a moment to sit and really look at each of your children. They are reflections of you, not only physically but also in character and intelligence, and in attitudes toward life, toward others, and toward themselves. Take time to admire each child. Your children are the products of your love, your time, your efforts, and your concern. You have done a good job! Take time every day to appreciate each child's individual qualities and development, to congratulate yourself and your spouse for a job well done, and to look upward and say, "Thank you!"

## SEND IDEAS

After reading *ParenTips,* I hope you will send me your ideas for my next book. With your children you have done things which didn't really seem to be unique learning experiences or brilliant solutions to problems, but they worked for you. Remember, ideas that seem natural to you may be novel to someone else. What works well in one family will work well in thousands of others, too.

Send your ideas and questions about life with children to:

Bonnie Burgess Neely
P.O. Box 595
Paris, Texas 75460

All letters become the property of Bonita Productions, Inc., and none can be returned. By sending the letters, the writers acknowledge that they may be edited or published (without names) at my discretion. I am sorry that the volume of mail prevents my answering letters personally.

If my feature does not appear in your newspaper, call your feature editor and request that your newspaper subscribe to *Formulas For Fun* by Beth Stone (my pen name) or *ParenTips* by Bonnie Burgess Neely. The editor may do so by contacting me at the above address.

Thank you!

# INDEX

# H

# I

# Q

# Having Your Baby...
# Raising Your Child

_____54382 **BABY NAMES FROM AROUND THE WORLD**
      Maxine Fields  $3.50

_____55187 **DR. SPOCK'S BABY AND CHILD CARE**
      Benjamin Spock, M.D. and Michael Rothenberg, M.D.
      $4.95

_____60156 **RAISING CHILDREN IN A DIFFICULT TIME**
      Dr. Benjamin Spock  $3.95

_____54152 **WHAT SHALL WE NAME THE BABY?**
      Ed. Winthrop Ames  $2.95

_____49637 **THE EXPECTANT MOTHER**
      Eds. Redbook Magazine  $3.50

_____60779 **NO NONSENSE NUTRITION FOR KIDS**
      Annette Natow and Jo-Ann Heslin  $3.95

_____55443 **ABC OF CHILD CARE**  Dr. Allan Fromme  $3.95

_____54302 **SLEEPLESS CHILDREN: A HANDBOOK FOR
      PARENTS**  Dr. David Haslam (trade)  $6.95

_____61119 **BOY OR GIRL?**  Dr. Elizabeth Whelan  $3.95

_____63346 **SLEEPLESS CHILDREN: A HANDBOOK FOR
      PARENTS**  Dr. David Haslam (rack size)  $3.50

_____53270 **NURSING YOUR BABY**  Karen Pryor  $3.95

_____49704 **PREGNANCY AFTER 35**  Carol McCauley  $3.95

_____43660 **TOILET TRAINING IN LESS THAN A DAY**
      Dr. Nathan Azrin & Dr. Richard M. Foxx  $2.95

_____81302 **SUMMERHILL: A RADICAL APPROACH
      TO CHILD-REARING**  A.S. Neill  $4.95

# Bringing Up A Brighter, Happier Child

The growth of a child's mind is a wonderful thing to watch. And it's even more wonderful when you've read up on the subject. Pocket books has a fine list of titles about the mental development of children written by prominent specialists in the field.

**If you are a parent, or soon plan to be, you'll want these books for your home library.**

_____ 63203  HOW TO RAISE A BRIGHTER CHILD
Joan Beck  $3.95

_____ 55442  IMPROVING YOUR CHILD'S
BEHAVIOR CHEMISTRY
Lendon Smith, MD  $3.95

_____ 55444  TEACH YOUR
BABY MATH  Glenn Doman  $2.95

POCKET
B O O K S

**Simon & Schuster, Mail Order Dept. CCB
200 Old Tappan Rd., Old Tappan, N.J. 07675**

Please send me the books I have checked above. I am enclosing $_____(please add 75¢ to cover postage and handling for each order. N.Y.S. and N.Y.C. residents please add appropriate sales tax). Send check or money order—no cash or C.O.D.'s please. Allow up to six weeks for delivery. For purchases over $10.00 you may use VISA: card number, expiration date and customer signature must be included.

Name _____

Address _____

City _____ State/Zip _____

VISA Card No. _____ Exp. Date _____

Signature _____ 617